Praise for *Repeat the Remarkable*

"One of the demons that overcomes individuals and organizations is complacency. This book contains the perfect antidote. Holley uses his IBM experience as a powerful metaphor for the value of discipline that ultimately inspires individuals and teams to soar to new heights."

—**Jack Zenger**, coauthor of the bestselling *The Extraordinary Leader* and *The Inspiring Leader*

"Perry is a natural teacher. You walk away from each chapter with renewed enthusiasm for personal improvement change. And it works for life as well as work!"

—**Jon Prial**, IBM WW Vice President, Sales Enablement (retired)

"In *Repeat the Remarkable* Perry reveals a step-by-step approach to not only achieving remarkable, but a proven plan for being able to repeat your remarkable performances. It is easy to fall into the trap of complacency after the big win. Perry lays out a plan to help you avoid that trap and become intentional about higher performance."

—**T. Falcon Napier**, founder, The Institute for Productive Tension

"I am endorsing this book because Perry is Remarkable. Thirty years of remarkable success is proof. If you too want to be remarkable and lead a remarkable team producing remarkable results—buy, read, and study this book. It's all in there."

—**Darren Hardy**, publisher of *SUCCESS*, CEO mentor, and *New York Times* bestselling author of *The Compound Effect*

"In today's economy, the pressure is ON to deliver better results every year. Perry artfully explores those internal motivations that inspire pervasive personal leadership. These motivations have the potential to transcend people from one-hit-wonders to truly remarkable 'chronic overachievers.' *Repeat the Remarkable* is full of great ideas to help you lead yourself and lead your team to greater heights."

—**Mike Madsen**, Vice President, IBM Software Group, Mid-Atlantic

"I found *Repeat the Remarkable* to be eminently practical and full of real-world advice. This book will affirm and influence those who are called to a leadership role. From chapters on clarity, authenticity, [and] leaders on cruise control to reaching the hallmark of remarkable and then repeating the effort, this book offers meaningful help for everyone at every rung of the leadership ladder."

—**Anne Bruce**, "The Authority on Motivational Leadership" and author of *Discover True North* and *The Manager's Guide to Motivating Employees*

"Finally a book that lays out the seemingly simple truths for someone wanting to be more than a one-hit-wonder. . . . Thank you, Perry!"

—**Bruce Mante**, IBM software sales executive

REPEAT
THE
REMARKABLE

HOW STRONG LEADERS

OVERCOME BUSINESS CHALLENGES TO

TAKE THEIR PERFORMANCE TO THE NEXT LEVEL

PERRY M. HOLLEY

New York   Chicago   San Francisco   Athens   London   Madrid
Mexico City   Milan   New Delhi   Singapore   Sydney   Toronto

1 2 3 4 5 6 7 8 9 0   DOC/DOC   1 9 8 7 6 5 4 3

ISBN 978-0-07-181118-7
MHID 0-07-181118-4

e-ISBN 978-0-07-181119-4
e-MHID 0-07-181119-2

Library of Congress Cataloging-in-Publication Data
Holley, Perry.
    Repeat the remarkable : how strong leaders overcome business challenges to take their performance to the next level / by Perry Holley.
        pages cm
    ISBN-13: 978-0-07-181118-7 (hardback)
    ISBN-10: 0-07-181118-4 (hardback)
1. Leadership. 2. Management. I. Title.
    HD57.7.H634 2013
    658.4′092—dc23

                                                                2013017763

While the author of this book is an employee of IBM, the opinions and information in the book are his own views and not that of the organization.

McGraw-Hill Education books are available at special quantity discounts to use as premiums and sales promotions or for use in corporate training programs. To contact a representative, please visit the Contact Us pages at http://www.mhprofessional.com.

This book is printed on acid-free paper.

■

This book is dedicated to those who model remarkable
in my life every day,
my wife, Bonnie, and my children, Katie and Paul.

■

CONTENTS

PART III: THE FUNCTIONALITY FOR REMARKABLE

PREFACE

A FRIEND OF mine once attended a performance of the famous group Cirque du Soleil. As you may know, Cirque du Soleil is an award-winning show featuring amazing feats of strength and dexterity all staged to music. The troupe describes itself as a "dramatic mix of circus arts and street entertainment."[1] When I asked my friend how he liked the show, he replied, "It was amazing—truly unbelievable."

"So, it was good?" I asked.

"No," he replied. "It went sailing way past being good. It was *truly remarkable*."

Sailing Past Good

Those three words, *sailing past good*, resonated in my mind, and I began to think about my life and my job at IBM. My mission there is to help salespeople, sales managers, and sales executives "sail past good."

Being good is no longer enough for anyone; and actually, it never was. If you stop at just being good, then you are more than likely losing ground with the truly top performers in your industry or area of specialization. Being good is the mere ticket of admission for being in business today.

Being remarkable, on the other hand, is what drives great results quarter after quarter, year after year. Being remarkable is what brings customers to you—instead of requiring you to go out and find them. Being remarkable activates that internal motivation we all need in order to go out every day and find a way to do it better, faster, and cheaper. Being and staying remarkable is what gets us out of bed in the morning, and it is what keeps us striving for more even when things are difficult.

Being remarkable differentiates us in the marketplace. Even though we all have the ability to achieve our own level of being remarkable, not all of us are willing to put in the effort to become remarkable. And once we achieve remarkable results, not all of us are willing to do the work to stay remarkable or repeat a remarkable performance.

From the "Remarkable We" to the "Remarkable Me"

As I write this, people around the world are trying to determine if they will come out of the worst global recession in the past 100+ years. Yet in the midst of this challenging economic time, my company—IBM— and many others have continued to grow and achieve great results.

Such success in trying times does not happen by accident. As author and speaker John Maxwell likes to say, "Everything rises and falls on leadership." If things are going well for your company or your team, it is because of good leadership. If things are not going so well or your team is not accomplishing its targets, it is because of poor leadership.

The good news is that you can grow as a leader. The bad news is that doing so requires diligent, purposeful work.

My reason for writing this book is to show you the characteristics of great leaders—and how these traits allow them to produce remarkable performances. Then, once we explore how they produce these remarkable performances, I will show you how they repeat their remarkable performances.

One thing I have learned in my years of leading teams is that *achieving* a remarkable performance is no guarantee of *repeating* a remarkable performance. In fact, it is a relative certainty that your team will *not* repeat remarkable performances if it is left on its own. Most people will have a "Hey, see what we've accomplished!" mentality that will keep them looking in the past instead of to the future. Back-to-back, remarkable team performances require strong and focused leadership.

A second purpose in writing this book is to help bridge the gap from what I call the "remarkable we" to the "remarkable me." What I have learned over my 30+ years of working with teams performing at a remarkable level is that it is incredibly easy to mistake *the team's* remarkable performance as *my own* remarkable performance. What I mean here is that I can easily be lulled into hiding my personal shortcomings when the team or company is doing very well. When things are good, I can get lost in the flurry of activities surrounding the great performance. I can confuse the *remarkable we* (the team or company) for the *remarkable me* and assume I can coast to the next great performance.

You Don't Have to Be Sick to Get Better

In reality, not everyone on the team has to be remarkable for the team to produce a remarkable performance. Just because my team produced a remarkable performance once does not mean that I am remarkable— or that it will happen again without my own commitment as a leader. As IBM continues to grow and achieve remarkable results, I must take personal responsibility for my own growth and ability to produce remarkable if I want to foster ongoing remarkable performances.

My friend Mark likes to say, "You don't have to be sick to get better." I often remind my audiences of this concept when I talk about a topic such as increasing personal or team performance. Although this little saying always gets a laugh, I always make sure that my listeners don't miss the point, which is this: even if you don't think you have a personal or team performance issue today, there are always areas where you could improve. Getting better when we don't think we need to get better is a great step toward truly being remarkable.

Thank you for joining me here on these pages. As we go through this journey together, I am going to encourage you to test your own ability to be remarkable and repeat remarkable as much as I am going to encourage you in how to lead remarkable performances in others. My commitment to you is that the end result will be worth your investment of time and energy. When we are done here, you will be able to define and execute the actions required for you to lead your team collectively—and each person individually—toward a remarkable performance.

ACKNOWLEDGMENTS

You CANNOT write a book about being and leading remarkable if you have not been exposed to and worked with remarkable people. I am blessed to have friends, family, and coworkers who model remarkable and who have been remarkable with their encouragement toward me about this project.

I would like to give special thanks to my new friends at McGraw-Hill for their trust and encouragement with this project. I would like to thank my editor, Donya Dickerson; my editing supervisor, Janice Race; and my production supervisor, Maureen Harper for their expertise in shepherding my book through the editorial and production processes. A special thanks to my copyeditor, Judy Duguid, for her skill in smoothing out my prose. I have learned from each of you more than I thought possible about what it means to convey a message through writing. You have truly been remarkable. And to my friend Jocelyn Godfrey, thank you for your remarkable insights and guidance.

To my dear friend and colleague Anne Bruce, thank you for encouraging me and pointing me in the right direction. I used to think that your writing 16 books (so far!) was an amazing feat, but after writing one book, I can now place your accomplishment at the top of my Remarkable Achievements list.

I would also like to thank the many mentors I have enjoyed— both those who have guided me in person and those who taught me through their writings. To my first in-person mentors—my parents, Horace and Sue Holley—there is no way that I can ever convey my love for you and my sincere thankfulness for the investment you have made in my life. Michael Bryant, thank you for investing in me. Gary

Gettis, your faithfulness astounds me. T. Falcon Napier, thank you for believing in me. Jeff Krider, thank you for being my "big fan" and always encouraging my art.

And to those who have mentored me through the pages of their writings—John Maxwell, Darren Hardy, Zig Ziglar, Brian Tracy, Robin Sharma, and Andy Stanley—thank you all for your remarkable examples.

No acknowledgment would be complete if I did not thank my bride of 30+ years, Bonnie, for her remarkable support of me and the many projects I continue to dream up. Through highs and lows, good times and growth times, your faithfulness to me and our family is truly my inspiration.

INTRODUCTION

Nothing is so common-place as to wish to be remarkable.

—WILLIAM SHAKESPEARE

THE YEAR was 1628, and the Swedish warship *Vasa* was to make her maiden voyage to join the other Swedish warships in the Thirty Years' War. An incredible 64-gun warship, the *Vasa* was larger than just about anything else found on the waters of Scandinavia in the seventeenth century. The *Vasa* had everything necessary to be a truly remarkable vessel with a truly remarkable story. But as I learned when I visited the Vasa Museum in Stockholm, Sweden, the story had a much less remarkable ending.

In a rush to get the *Vasa* into battle as quickly as possible, Swedish king Gustavus Adolphus gave orders for the ship to set sail on a specific date. Unfortunately, the design of the ship, with its impressive cannon decks, was built top heavy and required additional ballast to be added to the hull of the ship. The king's subordinates, not wanting to upset the king, failed to communicate that message and cut corners to get the ship to sea on the king's aggressive schedule. As the *Vasa* left Stockholm harbor and raised its mighty sails to catch the wind, the boat began to list, and water came pouring in the gun doors. The ship sank, killing many of the crew. Less than one nautical mile into her maiden voyage, the *Vasa* now rested on the floor of the sea.

I have been fortunate to visit Sweden many times and work with leaders all across the Nordic countries. I was excited to visit the Vasa

Museum to learn of this remarkable Swedish warship and all its great victories at sea. Instead, I found another example of how "remarkable" can be missed when leaders economize and allow their pride to move them past what they know to be good and true. What was meant to be majestic and awe inspiring became mediocre and a failure. What was meant to bring glory to a king and his country became an example of what not to do when remarkable is your goal.

Another Time and Another Ship

The year was 1997, and the naval warship U.S.S. *Benfold* was labeled one of the worst ships in the navy. By worst, it is said that the ship and crew were dysfunctional and unprepared to go to war. "The dysfunctional ship had a sullen crew that resented being there and could not wait to get out of the Navy," was how Captain D. Michael Abrashoff described the situation in his book titled *It's Your Ship.*[1]

In the 20 months that Captain Abrashoff was captain of the U.S.S. *Benfold*, he and the crew were able to take the ship from worst in the navy to first in the navy—and have their performance in naval exercises and war be described as remarkable. Captain Abrashoff learned early that his success in delivering remarkable performances would be heavily dependent on his skill as a leader and his ability to inspire his crew. He immediately began to set a tone of being more interested in achieving results than getting salutes. Traditional military command and control leadership was not what the *Benfold* needed. Abrashoff realized that his crew was closest to the action and procedures on the ship, and they therefore needed to feel that everything on the ship was their responsibility. This is how the *Benfold* watchword (and the title of the book) became *It's Your Ship.*

The differences between the *Vasa* and the *Benfold* are startling. In this comparison, there are many lessons for us to apply to our understanding of how to earn the label of "remarkable." As we progress through this book and its lessons about being and leading remarkable, we will unpack many of these rich truths.

A Message from the *Vasa* and *Benfold*

This tale of two ships provides us with many lessons when it comes to delivering and leading remarkable performances. As a leader, the message we want to embrace is:

1. **Focus on purpose.** On the *Vasa*, the crew was focused on pleasing the king; on the *Benfold*, the crew was focused on executing the mission at sea.
2. **Trust your crew.** On the *Vasa*, everything was viewed through the eyes of the leader (the king); on the *Benfold*, everything was viewed through the eyes of the crew.
3. **Lead by example.** On the *Vasa*, the king would dictate and manipulate; on the *Benfold*, the captain would collaborate and motivate.
4. **Never settle for "good enough."** On the *Vasa*, speed was of the essence, and "good enough" had to do; on the *Benfold*, the crew was inspired to go beyond standard procedure and minimum code and take ownership of every detail.
5. **Focus on results, not salutes.** On the *Vasa*, it was salute and stay mute; on the *Benfold*, crewmen were encouraged to speak up and right any wrongs.

The line between being remarkable and being a shipwreck is a very fine one for sure. It is so fine, in fact, that it is often undetectable. Rather than slipping into autopilot and doing things "the way they have always been done"—thus defaulting into repeating bad behaviors—we actually need to make conscious choices in order to change and achieve remarkable. Being able to recognize that being remarkable requires doing things differently is one of the greatest lessons you will find in this book.

When Being Good Is Not Good Enough

Average is over! Being "good" is not enough! What once got you noticed and moved you ahead, either as a company or as an individual, is not enough to get you ahead today. In these challenging times of the past three to four years, the landscape has changed in such a way that whether you buy or sell, lead or follow, build or service, the only way you can excel is to move your performance from good to remarkable. This is true for you personally, and this is true for your company. Now is the time for *remarkable*!

I love the word *remarkable*. Being remarkable goes beyond being really good at what you do. A lot of people are really good at what they do, but very few people are truly remarkable. A lot of companies are good at what they do, and they get by with just being good. But there are very few really remarkable companies. The ones that are remarkable are not interested in simply getting by; they are interested in making a difference—a difference in the lives of their customers, a difference in the lives of their employees, and a difference in their world.

IBM is one of those companies. I have been with the IBM Corporation for 25 of my 33 years in business, and I have seen this remarkable company grow and adapt to the constantly changing landscape of today's business marketplace. For more than 100 years, the IBM Corporation has been a leader in the highly competitive technology sector—a feat in its own right that is truly remarkable.

My role at IBM for the past 10 years has been to work with the sales and technical sales teams worldwide to improve performance and drive remarkable outcomes—both for individuals and for the teams. I work with leaders—those with a title and those without a title—to help them define and pursue what it means to be remarkable and drive remarkable performances. At this time in history, many

WHAT IS REMARKABLE?

Remarkable is the ability to consistently differentiate yourself or your company through the quality of your attitude, your actions, and your outcomes that drive undeniable value for your customers and cause others to sit up and take notice.

companies and individuals are trying just to keep their heads above water. I have noticed at IBM, however, that merely staying afloat is not now, nor has it ever been, an acceptable goal. Solving customer problems and being an indispensable part of the human experience while growing our revenue and improving our results is where the company is aiming, regardless of external circumstances. IBM's CEO, Ginni Rometty, calls it being essential. She is quoted as saying, "Make IBM the most essential company—to clients and to the world. It is a lofty goal, but that is our heritage." This means that during these trying economic times, we will need even more remarkable performances. In fact, remarkable will need to become more the norm than the exception.

But What About When Times Are Tough?

Great performances, like great companies, are not *made* in tough economic times; they are *revealed* in tough economic times. Remarkable individuals, like remarkable companies, don't shrink back in trying times; they push forward, finding opportunity where others see only challenge and risk. Remarkable performances and remarkable performers are not affected by economic conditions. Does that mean the economic conditions don't matter? No, it just means that in adverse economic conditions what average people or average companies do is not going to be enough to drive the results needed to compete in today's world. Average says, "Hunker down and stay safe." Remarkable says, "Set a goal, define a plan, and make it happen." Remarkable is a combination of attitude and action. Repeating remarkable becomes a way of life for which there is no easy substitute if you truly expect to differentiate yourself or your company.

Remarkable Can Be a Two-Way Street

Remarkable means doing something "worthy of notice or attention, or worthy of a remark."[2] One thing I have had to continually remind myself and others of when it comes to remarkable is that the notice or attention that marks our success does not come from us. We want the notice and attention to come from those we serve—our customers, our families, and our community! I can't tell you how many times I hear sales teams praising themselves for their own great performances. When you look at their results and ask them what their customers think, well, that's a different ball game.

If we are worthy of a remark, it needs to come from those whose remarks matter to us. If the only people you are causing to remark are on your team, then you are more than likely stuck in average when it comes to what your customer sees and experiences with you or your organization. I mentioned family and community earlier. I want to encourage you to consider what remarkable looks like in your personal life, not just your business life. Families and friends love being with remarkable people; so don't overlook an obvious opportunity to grow your skills toward remarkable in every area of your life.

Another interesting thing I have learned about being remarkable is that it does not have to be linked only to positive feelings or results. Remarkable can be a two-way street. I was on an airline flight once when the flight attendant, obviously having a bad day, told the passenger next to me that she would help him when she got the chance. For the time being, she told him that if he could just "chill out," she would really appreciate it. This caused our entire section of the aircraft to go silent and look up from what we were doing. The passenger she was speaking to exclaimed, "Remarkable," and I don't think he meant it in a good way. My suspicions were confirmed when the passenger asked the flight attendant for her name and the number of the flight.

Being remarkable involves more than simply being noticed. Being noticed is easy, but it is not always positive or productive. In the pages that follow, we want to focus on being remarkable and making a difference—a positive difference—in the lives of those we serve, whether customers, families, or communities. Being noticed is one thing; being noticed for a remarkable performance and making a positive impact in the lives of others is something else completely.

Repeating Remarkable

The ability to *repeat* remarkable performances is actually what got me started on this journey. At IBM, we have no shortage of amazing and remarkable performances. The trouble usually arises when the calendar changes from December to January, and we have to do it all again the following year—except this time we need double-digit growth. Many leaders struggle with seeing their teams do truly amazing things in one performance period only to have the teams fall apart when they move to the next performance period and encounter new sets of challenges. The natural tendency to relax and enjoy the victory has derailed many teams and kept them from repeating their remarkable performances. Later in the book, we will look at how to overcome the obstacles associated with repeating a remarkable performance.

"But I Want to Be Average!"

In all my years of mentoring and coaching individuals and consulting with companies and teams, I have never once had people tell me they desire simply to be average or mediocre. When I ask if they want to be remarkable or average, the response is always, "I want to be remarkable!" One hundred percent! No exceptions. The rub comes when we move past the talk of remarkable and start the walk of remarkable. What we will discuss in detail in the pages that follow are the specific steps required for someone both to be remarkable and to repeat remarkable. Whether you are learning for yourself or learning so you can lead others in repeating remarkable, there is a set of specific steps required to ensure that you and your team do not slide back into average. And as you will learn, sliding back into average is not really a noticeable, deliberate kind of thing. It happens slowly and is almost imperceptible over time—until one day you look up to see you have drifted from your goal of delivering a remarkable performance.

About This Book

My goal in writing this book is to provide you with a step-by-step plan for leading yourself and leading your organization in remarkable performances. As we discuss the Model for Remarkable and the various steps required for achieving it, I will also provide you with a set of tools and processes for developing a remarkable mindset in yourself and in everyone who serves with you in whatever business you run. Just as a side note, I have also used these principles in raising my children and instilling a remarkable mindset from an early age. I encourage you to consider these principles in all areas of your life.

Here is the flow of the book and how we will look into this important subject:

- **Part I.** The Model for Remarkable and the importance of establishing a strong foundation. I will define the two components of our foundation and show why it is important to get the foundation right for every remarkable performance. I will also walk through the important role of leadership when it comes to remarkable performances and look at a few of the factors that can cause detours from that path that leads to remarkable.

- **Part II.** The Model for Remarkable and the importance of establishing the framework that will make it possible to construct a performance worthy of others taking notice. I will unpack the four important parts of every remarkable performance and show how to make these a part of daily life.

- **Part III.** The Model for Remarkable and the importance of establishing the functionality that is the heart of everything you do. The functionality is the part of the Model for Remarkable that everyone else will see and experience. I will define these two important components and explain how to develop them in yourself and your team to ensure that remarkable is your defining characteristic.

Along the way, there will be a collection of tools and exercises to help guide and encourage you as you make your commitment to remarkable. I will tell you right now that being remarkable and, especially, repeating remarkable are *intentional choices* and do not happen without focused attention. If you expect to default into remarkable without making specific choices to get there, you will find yourself right in the middle of being average. For this reason, I want to encourage you to take the couple of extra minutes you will need to complete the exercises and learning aids so that you get the maximum benefit from this book.

At the end of each chapter, we will take a moment to review the *leader's conversation starter.* This will be your opportunity to assess your current situation and apply the lessons from the chapter in order to develop your own personal action plan or an action plan for your team. I encourage you to use the conversation starters with your team to discuss how to establish a culture for remarkable performances in your organization. If you do not lead a team at this time, use these discussion points as a way to establish a remarkable mindset in yourself that you will one day share with others.

Throughout the book, I will often reference "your customer," "your client," or "your audience" when I speak about those for whom we are being remarkable. Please consider these all synonymous. I recognize that we don't all have a customer per se, but we all do have an audience for our efforts. Whether your audience is your spouse and kids or the board of directors of a Fortune 100 company, I assume you can make the translation between customer, client, and audience.

As we make our way through this journey to being remarkable and repeating remarkable, I will be sharing stories with you from my own personal experiences. As leader of people at IBM to a teacher of people at IBM, I have learned many ways to ensure remarkable. Unfortunately for me and fortunately for you, most of these lessons came the hard way. In most cases, I missed remarkable and then had to circle back and try again to achieve it. You have the opportunity to learn from what I learned, so you don't have to make all those same mistakes—and that can be a very good thing!

Let's get started!

PART I

The Foundation for Remarkable

THE FOUNDATION

CHAPTER 1

Remark-*ability*: Enter Here— Laying the Foundation

Remarkability lies in the edges. The biggest, fastest, slowest, richest, easiest, most difficult. It doesn't always matter which edge, more that you're at (or beyond) the edge.

—SETH GODIN

BEING REMARKABLE at what you do is an aspiration that almost every person possesses. However, delivering and repeating a remarkable performance are achievements almost every person and every organization struggles with in one way or another. The steps are not necessarily difficult, but they do require a consistent, intentional, mindful approach if you hope to achieve the level of the truly remarkable. The world is full of one-hit wonders, like music groups that reach the top 100 charts with a hit song, but after their brief flash in the spotlight, they fade back into obscurity. That's not what I mean by being remarkable. Remarkable consists of delivering results that are not only beyond excellent—but also sustainable and repeatable. In our competitive world of bigger, faster, and cheaper, the achievement of remarkable is the differentiator that will move you and your business to the top. Being able to lead teams that deliver and repeat this rare, outstanding level of performance gives you a competitive advantage that will be difficult for others to match. To begin our journey toward creating consistently remarkable performance, let me share with you a story that I found to be truly remarkable.

A Remarkable Journey

One hundred years of anything is generally considered a remarkable accomplishment, but when that "anything" is competing in the global technology market, it is truly cause for taking notice. For the past 100 years, the IBM Corporation has been involved in such a remarkable journey. From its founding as the Computing-Tabulating-Recording Company (CTR) in 1911 with the merging of three separate businesses (Tabulating Machine Company [founded 1880], International Time Recording Company [founded 1900], and Computing Scale Company [founded 1901]), the International Business Machines (IBM) company has proved itself to be truly remarkable in both technology advancements and human resource accomplishments.

From its earliest beginnings, IBM established itself as a leader in every market it would serve. The company also took great pride in positioning itself as a leading place to work, pioneering workplace solutions decades before other companies or government regulations required them to do so. That's one of the hallmarks of remarkable people and remarkable companies—they don't wait for government regulations or others in the industry to innovate and find the way; they find the way and show others what is possible. This is the essence of what IBM has been doing for the past 100 years. Have there been setbacks and unremarkable times? Absolutely! It is very difficult for any individual or company to be remarkable all the time, but truly remarkable people and companies exhibit a key characteristic, and that is the ability to make course corrections that lead back to the pathway of remarkable performance.

When most people think of IBM, they typically think initially about the development of the first supercomputers. Depending on your age, you may think of the IBM Selectric Typewriter that enjoyed 75 percent market share and pioneered the word processing and desktop publishing markets. Or perhaps you recall the development of office copiers, the SABRE Airline reservation system, or IBM's leading role in the U.S. space program. There may even be areas that you are not aware of where IBM led the way with innovation and product development—things like the first artificial intelligence systems, hard disk drives, and the magnetic stripe on your credit card. IBM was also first to market in speech recognition, laser printing, LASIK eye surgery, and the UPC codes used at almost every retail checkout counter worldwide. And who can forget the first personal computer and portable personal computers? Most recently, Watson the supercomputer—the quintessence of IBM innovation and technology—competed on the popular game show *Jeopardy*, successfully defeating past champions in the challenging game show format. Whether you know it or not, the IBM Corporation has been a large part of each of our lives by bringing technology solutions to market that affect us all in one way or another.

The label of "remarkable" is not one that I, or you for that matter, should take lightly. While it is remarkable in many ways to bring innovative products and technology to the world in which we live, I also found it remarkable how IBM established itself as an international force in the midst of some of the most difficult external circumstances the world had ever seen. During the 1920s, IBM pioneered a new 80-column punch card that ran on its computing and tabulating machines. This expanded the amount of data that could be processed and was clear evidence that IBM saw a future in computing. Then, with IBM ramping up manufacturing of these tabulating machines, came the 1930s and with it the Great Depression. While most companies cut back or stopped manufacturing all together, IBM kept its plants running and stored the stockpile of machines in warehouses. When other companies were laying off their workforce, IBM maintained full employment and even instituted new employee programs to maintain high employee morale. It was during these tough and trying times that IBM developed such things as a 40-hour workweek for manufacturing employees, offering the first-ever salary plan for plant workers. IBM established the first employee training department and group life insurance. The leadership of IBM was definitely taking a risk, but the risk would pay off in remarkable ways.

As the Great Depression began to subside, the U.S. Congress passed what was to become known as the Social Security Act of 1935. With the enactment of this legislation came the immediate need for the government to collect, store, and calculate benefits for the 26 million citizens of the United States, and there was IBM with warehouses full of tabulating machines ready to go at a moment's notice. Some might call that lucky, but I call that remarkable: Remarkable leadership. Remarkable innovation. Remarkable results.

Creating a Model for Remarkable Performance

The remarkable journey of IBM and the stories of the men and women who have led that journey teach us that being remarkable and providing a remarkable performance is not something that happens by chance. What you will learn from the story of IBM and even your own personal experiences is this: being remarkable is not a gene, a birthright, or talent; being remarkable is a *choice*. Each one of us has the power to say, "I have decided to do whatever it takes not only to succeed, but to succeed in such a way that others (customers, employees, family, friends, colleagues, etc.) will sit up and take notice."

As a reminder from the Introduction to this book, here is my definition of *remarkable*:

> **Remarkable** is the ability to consistently differentiate yourself or your company through the quality of your attitude, your actions, and your outcomes that drive undeniable value for your customers and cause others to sit up and take notice.

To put that definition to work for you, I have built a model that will guide you in constructing every remarkable performance you deliver. The components of this model come from my observations and experiences through my years working at IBM and training IBM leaders. I have discovered that the qualities described in this model are a part of every remarkable performance. This model is made from the building blocks I have found to be necessary if your goal is to lead either a team, a company, or yourself into remarkable performances. When you or your organization can embrace and embody these building blocks, you will be able to consistently differentiate yourself and your organization through your remarkable results. And you will be able to replicate those performances to avoid being a one-hit wonder.

The model for remarkable performances consists of three main layers (see Figure 1.1). Each layer must be designed and developed for strength, but the exponential strength of the layers is revealed only when they are combined to deliver remarkable performances.

■ The first layer is the *foundation*. Nothing of any value will stand if the foundation is weak. While you don't always see the elements of the foundation, they are there—silently upholding everything else. The foundation is the first thing you construct when building for remarkable performances. Later in the chapter and in Chapters 2 and 3, we will discuss the *two key building blocks* in the *foundation* for remarkable that will make the foundation strong.

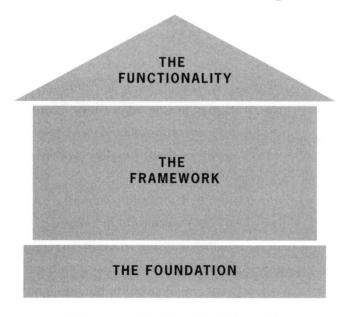

FIGURE 1.1 ■ **The Model for Remarkable**

- The second layer is the *framework*. The framework allows you to expand the structure so that it can house the important concepts of delivering remarkable performances. The framework is what you interact with on a daily basis—including the traits that support remarkable performance. In Part II of the book we will discuss the *four building blocks* in the *framework* for remarkable performances—similar to supporting walls in a home.

- And finally, the third layer of our model is the exterior siding and roof, which will bring *functionality*. Without the exterior, rain would get in and destroy everything you have worked hard to create. The exterior with which you wrap everything you do will protect your efforts and ensure that they are sustainable. The exterior provides the face that others see each day. In Part III of the book we will discuss the *two key building blocks* in the *functionality* for remarkable performances—similar to the siding and roof of a home.

These three layers comprise the characteristics of being remarkable, which—if properly developed—not only will support us but will also shelter us from the external circumstances and environmental forces that often derail our best efforts and leave us stranded in average or mediocre performances.

As I have worked with IBM leaders and their teams that are pursuing remarkable results, I also have found that there are a handful of "wrecking balls" that can keep even the best-performing teams from doing it right the first time and building remarkable. I will detail throughout the book a few of these wrecking balls that can destroy your efforts at becoming remarkable.

The Building Blocks of the Remarkable Foundation

As we explore the foundation, I will detail its two key building blocks. Think of these building blocks as being the mortar and stone that get mixed to create the concrete foundation.

Foundation Building Block #1: Know the What—the Outcomes—of Your Goal

The first main building block in the foundation of remarkable performances (see Figure 1.2) is *know the* what—*the outcomes—of your goal. That is, know and articulate what you are trying to accomplish.* If you do not know what you are trying to accomplish, you have no hope of achieving a remarkable outcome. At IBM, our leadership does an amazing job of painting the picture of what the desired outcomes will be. This starts with a five- to seven-year view of where the company will be, and it works its way through our fabric to the individual level of what is required of me to generate the results we need to generate. Remarkable results are not possible without a clear picture of what remarkable looks like.

The largest obstacle for most people and organizations wanting to provide remarkable performances is the failure to develop a clear understanding of what they are trying to accomplish. Creating and articulating a clear goal and complete understanding of the outcome

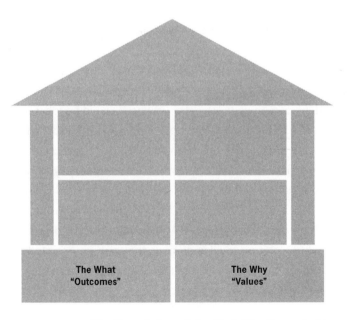

FIGURE 1.2 ▪ The Foundation of the Model for Remarkable

desired is the single most important component when it comes to leading or providing a remarkable performance. If you cannot articulate what a remarkable outcome looks like, from the customer's point of view, then you cannot possibly achieve it with any certainty. You may stumble on a remarkable outcome from time to time, but repeating remarkable will be almost impossible if you cannot articulate clearly what you plan to accomplish.

Sometimes the customer doesn't have a clear idea of what he or she wants. Or sometimes what the customer wants is only one piece of the greater process toward a truly remarkable outcome. That's where our skills come into play, as we have to find out how the ideal should or could function and what it will look like, even if we don't yet know

THE IMPORTANCE OF A POINT OF VIEW

When it comes to understanding the desired outcome for your audience, whether a customer, a community group, or your family, it is tempting to trust that others know exactly what they want to achieve. What often happens, however, is that many people (particularly customers) only see things from where they sit at particular moments. They know what they want based on their current vantage point. Remarkable performers provide *value* to their audience by having a point of view. This says, "I have been thinking about your business or situation as if it were my own, and if I were in your place, this is what I would be focused on—is this something you are focused on?" By having and expressing your point of view, you provoke the customer to think differently. This opens the door for more remarkable outcomes. To better serve your audience and to position yourself for remarkable, avoid simply being a yes-man and instead question thoroughly with the intent of exposing the possibilities for remarkable outcomes. Agreeing too quickly to a customer's proposed final solution could undermine the *value you bring* to the table and put you on the pathway of another average performance. Imagine the greater, long-term possibilities as you seek to answer customers' short-term requests.

the tactical solution to build it. We have to define "What is it that we want it to accomplish?" instead of "Which tool should we use to get this done today?"

When Thomas J. Watson, Jr., took over leadership of IBM in 1956 from his father, Thomas Watson, Sr., he immediately changed the management structure to position the company for growth. In 1962, to formalize the way he was already leading the company, he introduced what soon became known as the IBM Basic Beliefs. Those basic beliefs were *respect for the individual, customer service,* and *excellence.* It was Watson's view that this is how all IBMers would operate when selling and working with customers, prospects, and colleagues. Every IBMer was trained to always put the customers first and consider how we might best serve the customers in helping them achieve their objectives. The word *serve* was new to most people in the sales organization. One of the great truths that was being taught was that you can differentiate yourself and your organization by always having a point of view that helps your customers define possible outcomes. IBM still takes a lot of pride in helping customers achieve remarkable outcomes.

When I am asked to consult or provide a workshop for a client, my very first question of my sponsor is, "Please tell me what your end result for this session looks like. What do you want the people in attendance to be able to do, think, or say when we are through with the event?" If I know what I am aiming at, I can then begin to develop a map of how to get there. Note that I don't ask the customer, "How do you think I should accomplish it?" or, "What do you think I should do first?" That's "short-order cook" thinking, not chef think-ing. Rather, I ask the big-picture, end-result questions so that I can apply my unique strengths and skills to creating success. This might be this client's first workshop, and he or she could have a very narrow view of what a successful outcome looks like. I, on the other hand, have done many workshops and have a much wider view of what suc-cessful, even remarkable, outcomes might be. If I think back to the times when I have been less than remarkable in my performance, or to when the teams I was leading were struggling with being remarkable, I can trace my poor performance to not having a clear vision of the final outcome. We just started doing things hoping they would lead to successful results.

If you cannot articulate the goal (preferably in writing) so that everyone is in agreement on what is to be accomplished, then you set yourself up for an average performance—and not one worthy of anyone taking notice.

Foundation Building Block #2: Know the Why—the Values—of Your Goal

The second main building block found in our foundation for remarkable performances is to *know the why—the values—of your goal. That is, know why you personally are trying to accomplish the goal.* This is like adding stone or gravel to the mortar (the "what") so that it becomes strong.

Equally as important as knowing *what* you wish to accomplish is knowing *why* you are taking an action! People who deliver remarkable performances always have a clear understanding of why they are doing what they are doing. Explorer Ed Stafford's "why" involved being the first to do something (to walk the length of the Amazon River) that had not been done—a trait you find in many remarkable performances; but he also wanted to raise awareness of the climate issues that face the rain forests in South America. His why wasn't just about having *bragging rights* for being the first; his why also included helping a worthy cause.

You might be thinking that just being hired by a customer who is willing to pay me is "why" enough for any performance. And if you are looking to provide just "any" performance, I would agree with you. But remarkable individuals who provide remarkable performances for their clients tap into their own personal value systems for strength. Why? Doing so gives them the support they need to keep going when confronted with obstacles and tough times. And as I have learned, there is usually no shortage of obstacles and tough times.

How does this translate at work? If I am offered a speaking or consulting engagement, I always look for the connection between the desired outcome of my client (the what) and my strong desire to add value to the lives of others (the why). If I do not feel that I can provide that value in a definable way, then I do not have a strong enough why, and I will most assuredly end up providing only average results. If I am clear on how my skills and abilities combined with my desire to help others grow are applied to the task at hand, then I am pretty sure I have established the conditions where a remarkable performance can occur. Similarly, in your work, if you can apply the why of your task to what matters most to you, you will be much more engaged with the process of getting it done.

Over the past 25 years at IBM, there has been a real transition in the area of our why. While IBM has always been about innovation and the use of technology to help our customers be successful, the move to Smarter Planet branding has really raised the bar when it comes to our

IS YOUR WHY ENOUGH?

What if you are asked to undertake a task or project, but you struggle to see how it fits into what you perceive as your core strengths and skills? If you have proved yourself to be someone capable of remarkable performances, you will be sought out by others to help in areas you may not have previously considered. I was once asked by a friend if I would teach a lesson at his organization on cross-cultural communication. I knew that my friend admired my presentation skills and that he knew that I traveled internationally quite a bit. My thinking was that he had put those two things together and believed I was the perfect choice—international guy who can talk. I was not convinced. However, as I questioned him about the opportunity, I learned what he was trying to accomplish and why he thought I was the answer. I listened to his why and connected it to my why, and I found that there was not as much of a discrepancy as I had previously thought. My discomfort was based on the fact that I had never presented this topic before. He was giving me an opportunity to stretch and grow. Is your why enough? Look to your sponsor's why to see how it can connect to yours.

why. When IBM began to align its technology and solutions with not just helping our customers succeed but also helping our planet succeed, the company opened a door for remarkable to occur. As a leader in this organization, I now have the opportunity to help my team see beyond sales quotas and look to the bigger why of what we do—changing how our planet works.

You might be thinking, what if my why does not line up with the customer's desired outcome; should I reject the opportunity? Perhaps, but you might also use this as an opportunity to provide additional value to your customer by asking thorough questions about the outcome he or she is attempting to achieve. By tapping into your knowledge and experience in similar situations, you may be able to move the customer to an outcome that more fully aligns with your value system and personal strengths. This will provide the customer a superior outcome and will position you to be remarkable.

In the IBM story at the beginning of the chapter, you could see how it would be very easy to focus on a rich heritage of past successes. The IBM way, however, was to develop a strong why that would drive the company into even greater victories in the future. Positioning Smarter Planet and how we help clients grow and improve has been the why that IBM needs to move toward remarkable results. Focusing on things that have already happened is a huge waste of time and a distraction from where the focus really needs to be—on what lies ahead.

Many individuals struggle with overanalyzing the past. The key to establishing a strong foundation for remarkable is for you to focus on taking the lessons of yesterday and applying them to today and then moving into the future. Don't linger on the mistakes or regrets, but use what you learn from the past to make your future remarkable.

The IBM story and its 100-year history serve as a great reminder of what developing your ability to be remarkable is all about. As I compare this story with the challenges we face in our daily lives, I see a lot of similarities. I can imagine that there were many days when leaders at all levels of the organization had to put their heads down and plow through difficult circumstances. But once the mission had been accomplished successfully, those same leaders could enjoy their

WRECKING BALL TO GOAL ACHIEVEMENT: BEING A PRISONER OF THE PAST

It is okay that you have made mistakes. You can learn from what happened in the past, but you cannot be controlled by it. That would be like trying to drive a car looking in the rearview mirror—an obvious recipe for disaster. You are a product of your past, but you do not have to be a prisoner of it. Being a prisoner creates a wrecking ball to achieving your goals.

To move forward and avoid this wrecking ball, you must be determined to face the future. Remarkable performers have very short memories; they keep their eyes on where they are going, not where they have been. If you ever hope to be remarkable, you must always be looking forward toward the goal you are trying to accomplish.

success; their minds were no longer on those challenging days. Their only thoughts were of their remarkable accomplishment.

As Thomas Watson liked to say, "Every time we've moved ahead in IBM, it was because someone was willing to take a chance, put his head on the block, and try something new." Yet another characteristic of remarkable performers: they have complete belief that anything is possible if they are willing to work hard and throw themselves completely into the task of getting it done.

There Has to Be More to It Than That

You might be asking yourself, "Is that all there is to being remarkable? Do I simply need to know *what* my goals are and *why* I am setting out to achieve them?" The quick answer is no. What I have just laid out are the two *foundational* building blocks that all of remarkable is built upon. No matter how well you do everything else we talk about here, if you have not established a strong base to build your performances on, you will always come up short in your pursuit of remarkable performances. These two foundational building blocks hold up everything you do. They create the often invisible foundation for every remarkable performance you create. They are the strategic materials that must be in place before you intentionally create remarkable. Without them as your foundation, the structure of remarkable will fall—or worse yet, will never begin to rise.

CHAPTER 1 POWER POINTS

To review, here are the two foundation building blocks of remarkable performers:

1. Know the *what*—the outcomes—of your goal.
2. Know the *why*—the values—of your goal.

The foundation must be strong if you ever hope to consistently deliver remarkable performances. Taking a little time up front with your clients or audience will ensure that you can answer these two important questions about *what* the clients are trying to achieve and *why* you are the one to help them achieve it. As we saw in the IBM story, remarkable has come about by IBM's having the ability to be clear about what it does and how it can help others achieve specific outcomes. Likewise, developing a strong and undeniable *why* has been critical to IBM achieving the results it has achieved. All the innovation and product development would be meaningless if the values of serving customers, society, and the planet were not in place.

Leader's Conversation Starter

1. What are your core strengths that provide undeniable value to those you are trying to serve (customers, prospects, family, community)? What do you do better than anyone else?

   a. _____

   b. _____

   c. _____

2. What are your guiding values that support the work you do? Why do you do what you do?

   a. _____

   b. _____

   c. _____

CHAPTER 2

Clarity and the Leader
in the Mirror

Everything rises and falls on leadership.
—JOHN MAXWELL

I DON'T OWN a restaurant. I don't want to own a restaurant. I don't even know anyone who owns a restaurant. Yet I find myself watching and being completely engrossed in the Food Network television show *Restaurant Impossible*.[1] I enjoy watching as the host, Chef Robert Irvine, tackles problem after problem in a restaurant he has been called in to save. It is not just a restaurant show. The subject is restaurants, but the lessons are universal and mainly relate to leadership, discipline, and results.

What I find fascinating about this television show is that every one of the failing restaurant owners started their business because they felt like they had a remarkable product or service that should be shared with the world. In many cases the restaurants have been in the family for a generation or two. In every situation they are failing, and the reasons all point to leadership. Chef Robert always uncovers some combination of the same three or four problems every time he arrives on the scene. I think there is a lesson here for every person desiring to lead remarkable teams to deliver remarkable performances.

The Importance of a Strong Foundation

As I discussed in Chapter 1, our model for remarkable performances has three parts, the *foundation*, the *framework*, and the *functionality*.

Having a strong foundation is incredibly important if we ever hope to consistently provide a remarkable experience for our clients, family, and community. Knowing the what and the why establishes a base that will support the other components of our model. One thing that has been clear to me in the *Restaurant Impossible* episodes that I have seen is that people think they know what they are trying to accomplish and why they are trying to accomplish it, but it does not take very long to see that in most cases the leaders have drifted away from what they originally set out to do.

In my years at IBM, I can see a direct correlation to the questions that Chef Robert asks each restaurant owner and the success of the business. When you look at the history of IBM and compare the remarkable times with the nonremarkable times, you can see immediately the relationship between knowing what you are in business to do and why and the overall success of the business. In the 1990s when IBM struggled for survival, it became apparent that we had drifted from our core values. We were trying to be everything to everybody. We were attempting to cover the immense technology market from top to bottom, and it was causing an enormous distraction that kept IBM from focusing on what it did best. Much like a restaurant owner that continually adds new food items to the menu, IBM just kept branching into more and more areas of technology. The overriding result was that we became average at a lot of things and remarkable at nothing. When new leadership arrived, one of the first tasks it undertook was eliminating lines of business that were keeping IBM from the remarkable results it had once enjoyed. Returning to a solid foundation of doing a few things with excellence was the first step in returning IBM to remarkable.

Why Are We Doing This?

The first question Chef Robert asks when he meets a restaurant owner is, "Tell me about your restaurant. Why did you start this business?" The answers range from "Because it was handed down to me from my parents" to "It seemed like a good idea at the time." What is usually revealed is somewhere along the way the owner had a vision and a passion for cooking and wanted to share that talent with others. Chef Robert then asks, "So, what happened?" At this point there are usually tears as the owner explains that this is no longer fun and he or she doesn't know when or why the fun stopped. The reason the restaurant owner started the business is no longer the reason he or she is still in the business. At some point it stopped being about delivering a remarkable experience to the customers. Somewhere along the way it became a job, and the focus of the owner shifted from remarkable to survival.

This Is Not What I Signed Up For

Chef Robert, after spending a few minutes with the owner to hear the original vision, goes on to spend a few minutes with the restaurant staff. What he usually learns from the people working there is that the restaurant has slowly changed over time, and even though they don't agree with the changes, it is not their place to say anything. This is not what they signed up for, but it's not their problem. Many times the employees are family members who feel that their input is not appreciated, and so they just salute and stay mute. There are usually more tears as people who care a great deal for the owner tell of their pain in watching the situation deteriorate over time.

When you see the condition of the restaurant when Chef Robert arrives, you are amazed that anyone goes there to eat. Once he inspects the kitchen area, you are amazed that no one has died from eating there. Detail after detail of running a successful restaurant has been ignored, some of them for years. How did it get this bad? Did the owner lose his or her passion for the business? No. In almost every case you can see the sadness the person feels for having allowed things to get this bad. But in every case people seem blinded to how to turn the ship around. In most cases they are thousands and thousands of dollars in debt, and yet they will continue to throw more good money after bad in hopes that conditions will improve. The message that Chef Robert is there to deliver is that they need to wake up and make some difficult changes if they ever hope to deliver remarkable products and services again.

REMARKABLE IMPOSSIBLE

If you could call in a reality television star to assess your business for the possibility of being remarkable, what would he or she find?

TRUE   FALSE

_____   _____   You seem to be confused on what your value is to your customers.

_____   _____   Your customers do not see the value, as it relates to them, of what you do.

_____   _____   You lack focus, and you are trying to do too many things.

_____   _____   The level of communication of your team is poor.

_____   _____   Not everyone on the team is clear on what we do best.

Everything Depends on Leadership

The quote at the beginning of this chapter pretty much sums up the situation at the restaurants in this television show, at IBM, and most likely in your place of work—everything rises and falls on leadership. The problems that Chef Robert uncovers are all related to the leader.

- The food tastes bad—the leader has not empowered, trained, or instructed the people who prepare the food.
- The menu has too many items—the leader has allowed the vision of the restaurant to morph into seven other things that were never intended to be.
- The service is terrible—the leader has allowed the employees to become disconnected to the vision of what this business is all about.
- The decor is out of date and dirty—the leader has focused on other things he or she thinks are more important than the first thing the customer sees.

In every case, in every business, everything rises and falls on leadership. What kind of a leader are you? If a Chef Robert type of person for your industry showed up at your office, would he be shocked and surprised at what you had allowed to happen? Or would he shake your hand and congratulate you on how you are running your business? It is a choice you are making every day whether you know it or not. In the case of IBM and of every restaurant that Chef Robert visits, drifting from what made the business great did not happen overnight. It was a slow and steady decline over a period of years. The seemingly insignificant decisions made consistently over time were compounding negatively and leaving the business in danger of closing. To be consistently remarkable requires conscious, intentional choices that compound positively.

IBM has been able to maintain its reputation and market position for over 100 years. All the leaders are told in no uncertain terms that whether IBM succeeds or fails is up to them. Strong leadership will bring strong results. To make sure strong leadership occurs, IBM does three things to strengthen every leader's position:

- **Enablement.** Every leader at every level in the organization is expected to complete management and leader education. The content of this education ranges from how to manage the process to how to lead people.
- **Mentor/coach.** Leaders at IBM are expected to have a mentor/coach that they meet with on a regular basis. The purpose of these meetings is to allow the individuals being mentored to openly discuss the challenges they face and get input and ideas from someone who has gone before them. New leaders are never left to figure it out on their own.
- **Accountability.** It probably goes without saying, but accountability is the key to good leadership. At IBM, leaders are held responsible for the progress of their part of the business and the progress of the people who work for them.

Maintaining a strong leadership culture is essential to establishing a foundation for delivering remarkable performances. Without it, organizations are prone to drifting, and drifting never ends up in the remarkable category.

They Just Do What They See Me Do

I once saw a cartoon that showed two managers from a local business walking together. One manager said to the other, "It doesn't matter how many times I tell my people what to do, they just keep doing what they see me doing." John Maxwell, in his book *The 21 Irrefutable Laws of Leadership,*[2] calls this the law of the picture—people do what people see. Many leaders fail to recognize this law and expect their followers to do what they are told, not what they see. This area of the IBM leadership culture falls under the "accountability" heading. All leaders are held accountable for their results and for the example that they put in front of their team. You won't find a team inside IBM where the leader is not working as hard as or harder than the team he or she leads. Whether times are good or bad in the economy, regardless of the part of the world where you work, leaders are held accountable for the results they are driving.

Let's apply the leadership concepts to you and your business. I would like to introduce you to four concepts for leading remarkable performances and challenge you to consider each component as it relates to how you lead your teams and your business.

> *Leaders aren't born, they are made. And they are made just like anything else, through hard work.*
> **—VINCE LOMBARDI**

But before we get to the four concepts of clarity, openness, straight talk, and focus, let's deal with a question that many people ask when the topic of leadership is discussed. That question is, "What if I don't lead anything or anyone—what if I am not a leader?" That's a great question, and I am glad you asked. I consider leadership to be your ability to positively influence others. You do not have to have a title or a team to be an influencer of others. We will talk more about this in the coming pages, but the most important person you lead is you. By leading yourself well, you begin to build influence in the lives of those around you. It is only a matter of time before you will be asked to lead a team or a business. But even if that is not your desire, you can still build your skills around leadership and personal influence.

There has been a lot written over the years about the various levels of leadership. One thing that everyone agrees on is that the lowest level of leadership is positional. This means that people follow you because they have to, because of your position or title. In every other level of leadership, people follow you because they want to. They see something in you that makes them want to be a part of what you are doing. I have not found one leader of remarkable performances that is a level-one leader. In every case, remarkable leaders have great influence with their followers, and those followers follow because they want to, not because they have to.

Remarkable Leadership

Where you find strong leadership at IBM and at other successful companies that are driving remarkable results, you will find a culture of leadership that embraces four core components of remarkable leadership. As you can see in Figure 2.1, the components that I find important for leading remarkable performances are *clarity, openness, straight talk,* and *focus*. Where these items come together is where you will find remarkable leaders.

Clarity—Make Vision IKEA-Clear

Clarity precedes mastery.
—ROBIN SHARMA

The quickest way to undermine a remarkable performance is to be unclear on what you are trying to accomplish. As you recall from Chapter 1 and the Model for Remarkable, the foundation layer was about knowing what you are trying to accomplish. That same concept is magnified in importance when you are the leader. Your job is to

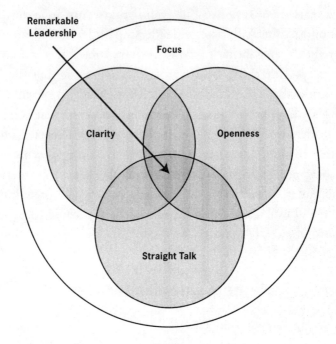

FIGURE 2.1 ■ **Remarkable Leadership**

paint so clear a picture for your team and for yourself that there is absolutely no doubt what the end result will look like.

I compare this to building a piece of furniture purchased at IKEA.[3] If you have not had that pleasure, trust me; it is terrific. You purchase a bedroom dresser drawer set that comes in a box about three inches thick. When you open the box and pour out the contents, you immediately begin to panic. There are dozens of parts and dozens of nuts and bolts. Now, I am a guy, and so I would not normally look for the instructions; but since this is a five-foot-high dresser drawer set that came in a box only three inches thick, I am puzzled by how complex this is beginning to appear. So I grab the instruction booklet, yes booklet, and begin to turn the pages. News flash: there is not one printed word on the instruction pages. Instead there are pictures of the parts and how they go together—one step per page. The pages even include pictures of how they do *not* go together. The booklet starts with a picture of the finished product and then a picture of all the parts you will use, and then it tells you to get started. This is how I want to communicate to my team; I want to be IKEA-clear. I want the members of my team to know what my expectation is of the finished product, and then I want to let them work through the pages to accomplish that outcome.

Looking back at the *Restaurant Impossible* examples given earlier, I notice that, without exception, when the restaurants found themselves in trouble, it was because the owners stopped communicating their expectations for the business. They assumed that everyone knew what to do and would do it. What they failed to realize is that their people were watching them. Your people are always watching you, whether you know it or not, and they will do what they see, not what you say.

At IBM, the leaders who are most successful have a defined communication plan for their team. The most successful use a combination of team meetings (virtual or face-to-face) and one-on-one discussions. When I have felt most connected to the mission of the team and direction of the company was when I worked for an individual who spent some time each week speaking with me one-on-one. I am often amazed by the number of leaders who don't do this. Set some time each week to speak with and encourage the people who work for you. It will make a positive difference in your business. For example, here is a plan that, though incredibly simple, goes to the heart of excellent communication across the organization:

- **One-on-one.** Spend at least 30 minutes a week speaking one-on-one with the people who report directly to you. During this time, spend a few minutes up front inquiring about them personally (what's going on in their life, how is the family, etc.). Next, ask them what they have for you today. This is their chance to tell you about what they are working on and ask questions. Next, tell them what you have for them today. This could be work assignments, follow-up on earlier work assignments, or a review of upcoming calendar events. Finally, close with a word of encouragement and thanks for the job they are doing.

- **One-on-team.** Spend at least 30 to 60 minutes a week meeting with your team. This is an excellent time to highlight results, review strategy and direction, examine execution challenges, etc. You might also consider bringing attention to specific members of the team for the work they are doing. You might also consider having a different team member each week present a 3- to 5-minute overview of a project or accomplishment. Always ask if anyone has anything he or she would like to share with the team. As you close the meeting, whether face-to-face or in a conference call, share a word of encouragement and thank the members of the team for their hard work and focus on the business.

▪ **One-on-organization.** If you have a larger organization, it is also good to conduct monthly calls with the entire team. The content for these calls is similar to the one-on-team calls above, where strategy, direction, and expectations are communicated.

UNDERSTANDING AND BEING UNDERSTOOD

Author and teacher Brian Tracy said, "Accept complete responsibility both for understanding and for being understood," So many times I find that I expect others to understand me, and I am frustrated when they do not. Follow this model to increase clarity and reduce frustration:

Step 1: Take complete responsibility. If there is a lack of clarity, it is my fault. To build strong relationships and increase the effectiveness of my communication with others, I need to take *complete* responsibility for our conversation.

Step 2: Focus more on understanding. Even though I feel I am an understanding person, in communication sometimes I fail to listen with the intent to understand. I am too focused on forming my response. Understand before you respond.

Step 3: Focus less on being understood. We all want to be understood, which is why this need often eclipses the focus on understanding. Yielding your "right" to be understood will free you to focus on truly understanding. The truth is that if I focus more on understanding, I am less likely to have a strong need to be understood.

CHAPTER 2 POWER POINTS

The focus of this chapter has been on ensuring that you are the kind of leader who can consistently lead a team or yourself into remarkable performances. As was stated at the beginning of the chapter, everything rises and falls on leadership, and it is up to you to do your part to be that remarkable type of leader. Some things worth remembering include:

- Remarkable leaders provide clarity of objectives.
- Remarkable leaders keep the focus on the desired outcomes.
- You can lead without a title. You don't have to hold a position of leadership in the organization to be a leader. True leaders lead by positively influencing others.
- How you communicate with your followers is an important part of reaching remarkable.

Leader's Conversation Starter

To understand how clear your goals are for your team, ask each member of the team to answer the following questions. Have the individual team members share their thoughts with the team.

1. I am very clear on what we are trying to accomplish as a team.
   _____ True   _____ False
2. One thing that would increase clarity of our mission would be for us to _____

_____

CHAPTER 3

What Keeps People from Following My Lead?

Leaders, by virtue of their authority, exert a disproportionate impact on the mood of those they supervise.

—TONY SCHWARTZ

THE SECOND concept for building a foundation that will enable remarkable performance is to become a leader who embraces openness in your communication style (see Figure 3.1). Dr. John Maxwell once shared that as leaders we have a choice every time we come in contact (phone, e-mail, face-to-face) with our followers. We can choose to do one of two things: we can motivate them and have them persevere through whatever struggle our organization is facing. Or we can manipulate them with our words to get what we want to help make us look good to our up-line leadership.

The funny thing is that most leaders don't really see this choice to motivate or manipulate as a choice. We do this so seamlessly that it has become almost a default response to the stimuli coming at us in our day-to-day environment. I almost wrote "our day-to-day work environment," but as I have learned, you can use this same technique with your family and friends in your home or in your community. It's a choice for sure, and we need to wake up to that fact while we still have followers and families.

When I see this characteristic in others, it usually comes in the form of them doing more telling than asking. They are usually in a hurry, and they need something immediately. Now, I believe leaders should be able to tell their people to do something without playing 20 questions, but I find that when I come storming into their space (face-to-face or electronically) and start demanding something without showing respect for who they are as individuals and who they are as contributors to our organization, I have just squandered an opportunity to motivate them to even higher levels of performance. You can't motivate and manipulate at the same time; it's one or the other. Choose manipulate too many times in a row, and you begin to push your people away and they disengage. When they disengage, performance drops.

The most lasting form of motivation in most individuals is the kind that comes from within them: an intrinsic motivation. This intrinsic motivation is driven by how they feel about themselves in connection with their work, with their boss, or with their environment. As a leader, are you responsible for someone's self-esteem or self-image? Of course not, but you can help inspire someone's self-esteem and self-image by communicating with them in such a way that increases

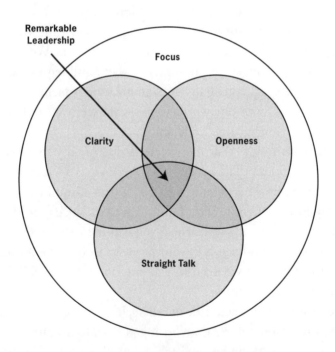

FIGURE 3.1 ▪ Remarkable Leadership

their intrinsic value and thus increases their motivation to contribute significantly to your organization. Motivate me and I engage. Manipulate me and I disengage. Engagement drives performance.

One of the areas of focus for leaders at IBM is engaging and retaining our top talent. We have learned over the years that people go and stay where they feel valued. We have also learned that if we spend all our efforts on managing the business instead of leading the people, the value people feel decreases, and the potential for them to leave increases. If you hope to lead your team to consistently deliver remarkable performances, then you need to realize that you have a lot to say about whether people feel valued in their work or not. Author Brian Tracy says, "Every time you smile, you greet, you thank, you praise, you encourage, you recognize, you admire, you listen—you increase someone's value and you increase their motivation and you increase their performance."

Constructing a Climate for Remarkable

Often leaders can feel that this is way too soft an approach. You can almost see them flinching when "concern for your people" is discussed. It's worth remembering that leadership is a people business, and one thing you can count on with people is that they always go where they feel valued. This does not mean that you have to be all soft and mushy, but it does mean that you need to balance openness and concern.

At IBM, when we train a manager, at any level in the organization, a lot of time is spent on the climate you create as a leader. Organizational climate is how it feels to the individual to work in your organization. It is important because the climate you create influences how your team members respond to you and how they apply themselves to the work to be done. Many leaders, when they come into the IBM training, believe that climate is something that occurs through outside forces, i.e., the economy, the recent election, industry regulation, etc. When they leave the training, they understand that the biggest determinant of climate is the leader. That is why you often hear it said that employees do not quit a company; they quit a person. Most of the people who work for you can endure bad economies and bad elections and bad industry regulation if they feel valued and relevant to you and what your organization is trying to accomplish.

Whether you work in the business world, the classroom, or the home, this is a truth that applies to all communication. When you can balance openness and straight talk with genuine concern for the individual, you provide an environment for people to grow and perform at their very best.[1]

Openness means being honest and frank with your boss, your team, your students, or your children. You tell people how they are really doing. You share both the good and the bad of what you see going on in their life. Concern means showing that you care for them personally—who they are and what they mean to you. You reassure them of their value to the organization and to you personally.

The secret is to have a balance. If the climate you provide as a leader is all openness, then it will not take very long for the individuals involved to feel judged, angry, embarrassed, and beat down. On the other hand, if the climate you provide is all concern, then there is never a time of accountability, of having blind spots revealed, of hearing how we can improve. In short, there is no opportunity for growth to occur in an environment where no gaps are identified and talked about.

An example of how this would play out in your home might look like this:

- An *all-concern* environment would have a child being constantly reminded of her value and worth without ever being talked to about her bad attitudes or actions.
- An *all-openness* environment would have a child being constantly reminded of his bad attitudes and actions without ever being told of his value and worth.

I personally witnessed a great example of what a balanced approach looks like when my good friend Kevin was being told by his doctor what the extent of his brain hemorrhage had been. The doctor started by showing great care for Kevin and commenting on how far he had come in the recent days and weeks. But then he shifted to a direct explanation of what was ahead for Kevin. It was not easy to hear, but we did not go away with unreasonable expectations. We had hope, but we knew there was work ahead. We wanted the truth about the situation, but the delivery needed to be packaged in care and with feeling. Too much concern and we might have left the doctor's office thinking all is well and good with Kevin's health. Too much frankness and we would have left the doctor's office feeling depressed and hopeless. It's a balance.

This is the exact approach we recommend for an IBM manager when providing an annual performance evaluation. Begin with showing care for the individual and conclude with being straightforward about the performance. Often, leaders can be so focused on delivering the performance evaluation that they lean way too far to the candid side of things. This can come across to the employee as cold and impersonal, especially if the evaluation is less than stellar. We encourage leaders to make every interaction with a team member personal and impactful by balancing concern with openness. If you favor one over the other, you are going to have team members leave your presence feeling either they can do no wrong or they can't do anything to please you. Neither extreme is a healthy place to be. Balance is the answer.

To position yourself as a leader who can lead remarkable performances, you must seek out the balance when dealing with your team or your followers. This adds to the clarity that a team needs around expectations and desired outcomes. To find the right balance in any situation, there are two steps that each of us can take to ensure we position our teams to succeed.

It's About the Balance

Whether you are leading a business or leading your home, the first step to staying balanced in your communication is to *develop trust by always being consistent*. When we let our emotions run unchecked, we are telling others that the circumstances are more important than they are. If it is a good circumstance, then I am in a good frame of mind and I communicate good things. If the circumstance is bad, then I am in a bad frame of mind and I communicate bad things. When I was working a part-time job during college, I worked for a guy who had terrible swings in emotion depending on what was happening in his personal life or in the business that day. Before any of us on the team would go into his office, we would check with one another for the most up-to-date reading of his emotional state. Because he was so emotionally inconsistent, we had to walk on eggshells until we could figure out if this was a good day or a bad day. This caused an environment of distrust. The members of your team cannot move toward remarkable performance if they always have to worry about you and your mood swings. Be consistent in how you deal with your team regardless of the current circumstances. Place people above circumstance, even if the people caused the circumstance. This will develop trust and a consistent approach to both the openness and the caring side of your communications.

> *You're never as good as everyone tells you when you win,*
> *and you're never as bad as they say when you lose.*
> —LOU HOLTZ

Second, *never deliver openness without leading with some concern.* No matter what the message you need to convey to a team member, always put the person first. Just to be clear—person first, message second. Always lead with concern in order to reassure the people you are speaking openly to that you approve of them personally and you only want them to improve and grow. Then move into the candid part of your message. Most people I have worked with know that they can be better at what they do, but often the leaders they are under refuse to be forthright about what they need. Then when a leader directly addresses a problem, people miss the lesson because they are worried that the leader has it in for them. With a little balance the followers are positioned to hear the straight talk and apply it to improving their performance. When people know you care about their growth and development, they can take about anything you can throw at them. It's when we start throwing without them knowing we care that we get into trouble and actually do damage to our team.

One way remarkable leaders can successfully deliver a tough message to a person on their team is to *use themselves as an example.* The problem most people have with straight talk is that it sounds like they are being lectured by a superior person. Using your own shortcomings as a basis for the conversation lets them know that they are not the first to need this talk and that you can relate to where they are coming from. This approach also helps with building trust between your team members and you. If you are willing to share how you have struggled in a similar way, then they can know that you are truly interested in their growth and development. When you make their shortcomings the focus while making yourself look perfect, you have positioned a wall between you and your audience that will be difficult for many people to overcome.

Communicating When the Stakes Are High

The third concept that I think is incredibly important for leaders who desire to lead remarkable teams into remarkable performances is the ability to communicate when the stakes are high (Figure 3.1). I was teaching a lesson to a large group of sales managers in Europe when I asked them to raise their hands if they currently had a situation on their team where they needed to deliver a difficult message about an employee's performance. In response, 70 percent of the hands in the room went up. Then I asked the audience to keep their hands up if this situation was greater than one month old. Over 90 percent of the hands stayed up. The vast majority of audience members had a difficult message to deliver, but they were in no hurry to deliver it even though it meant an improvement to their business. Why is that?

When training IBM leaders, one problem area that we see is leaders who have trouble communicating when the stakes are high. By "stakes are high" I mean that the message being delivered is not necessarily a positive or encouraging one, and it has the potential to have a negative effect on the people receiving the feedback. This feedback could be about their performance, a correction of their behavior, or an assessment of the attitude they recently displayed. Truth be told, most of us would rather just avoid those direct and often painful conversations even though we know that by doing so the problem or situation will more than likely repeat itself in the near future.

Whether you are in the corporate world or are a schoolteacher, a parent, or a spouse, you will often have the need to engage in difficult conversations with those you live and work with. Your ability to have these conversations in a positive and constructive way will determine the long-term strength and success of these relationships. Most leaders have struggled at some point in their career with doing these conversations poorly or not at all, which leads to continued avoidance. This avoidance allows for further problems, and the cycle continues. You cannot lead anyone to remarkable without confronting issues with your team head-on.

Developing Your Ability for Straight Talk

In their outstanding book *Crucial Conversations,*[2] authors Kerry Patterson, Joseph Grenny, Ron McMillan, and Al Switzler outline a proven technique for handling conversations when the stakes are high. The book outlines several techniques for having these important conversations with individuals on your team, but the real lesson to be learned is that you need to start with your own motivations and pay close attention to the environment you are providing for an honest conversation. Does the other party feel safe enough to have an open, honest dialogue, or does the person feel threatened and choose to just stay quiet?

The reason why many leaders want to avoid having the difficult conversation is because they see it as some sort of competition that they are trying to win with another human being. The secret to getting off to a good start in any difficult conversation is to be clear about your desired outcome. You cannot change another person—you can only change you—so stay focused on your end goal and avoid the desire to be right, to make yourself look good, or to just plain win.

An IBM best practice here is to ask our leaders to separate the problem from the person. Focus on fixing the problem, not on fixing the person. You cannot "fix" another person; only the person can do that.

So don't get tangled up in a confrontation trying to do so. Instead, focus on the issue and how correcting the issue can help the person (and the organization) be better. One of the reasons that many leaders avoid the difficult conversations they know they should have with their people is because they think they are there to change the person. When we get them focused on changing the behavior and not the person, their attitude about having the difficult conversation improves immensely.

The second big truth to apply is to pay attention to the safety of the environment you are providing. An unsafe environment is one where the people you are confronting feel that you are out to get them or that you merely want to prove that you are right. Evidence of this unsafe environment comes in the form of what the authors of *Crucial Conversations* call "silence or violence." If you notice that the people you are speaking with go silent and become withdrawn, you can pretty much

ANGRY COMMUNICATION

Most of us can make our way through our work careers without ever having to engage in an angry exchange with a coworker, but it does happen. More than likely you reserve your really angry exchanges for those closest to you in life—your family. To avoid or recover from an angry exchange, here are some actions you can take:

- Put the relationship above the issue.
- Be angry with a circumstance or an action, but not with the person.
- Lower your tone and reject the urge to raise your voice.
- Agree on the goal you are trying to accomplish.
- Agree on reality—what is your starting point?
- Work together to decide on two to three options to move forward.
- Decide together which option you will try first.
- Agree that if that option does not work, then you will try another option.
- Recover well—don't let anger stand between you and an important relationship.

be sure they do not feel safe in opening up to you. The same is true if they adapt some sort of aggressive, argumentative approach with you.

If you notice the signs in the person you are confronting that he or she feels the environment is unsafe, you must establish mutual purpose and mutual respect. Mutual purpose says that we are working toward the same goal—not to have one person win or be proved right, but to improve a situation or achieve some change. Mutual respect says that we keep this about the action or behavior and not about the person. The message "I respect you, but I don't approve of your behavior" is much different from making someone feel you don't approve of him or her.

When a leader can approach every conversation, difficult or otherwise, with humility and an "others" orientation, it goes a long way to making for a safe environment. Once safe, we can each share from our individual points of view and work quickly toward resolution. Any attempt by the leader to control the other person, try to change the other person, or somehow make himself or herself look good does nothing more than shut the door to possible resolution. When leading remarkable performances, it is imperative that you and your team have clarity around your mission and the permission to speak in a direct and straightforward manner to avoid misunderstandings.

CHAPTER 3 POWER POINTS

You can ensure that you are the kind of leader that can consistently lead a team or yourself into remarkable performances by recalling the following:

- Remarkable leaders provide openness of communication.
- Remarkable leaders provide straight talk.
- Remarkable leaders keep the focus on the desired outcomes.
- How you communicate with your followers is an important part of reaching remarkable.

- Balance openness with concern.
- Motivate; don't manipulate.
- Straight talk builds trust with teammates. Develop your ability to communicate with people when the stakes are high.

Leader's Conversation Starter #1

To understand the level of openness your team feels, ask each member of the team to answer the following questions. Have the individual team members share their thoughts with the team.

1. I feel that we have an incredibly open communication policy on this team.
   True _____ False _____

2. One thing I would do to increase openness in our communication would be for us to _____ _____
   _____
   _____

Leader's Conversation Starter #2

To understand the comfort level of the members of your team to say what is on their minds, ask each member to answer the following questions. Have the individual team members share their thoughts with the team.

1. I feel that I am able to say what I think and feel to this team.
   True _____ False _____

2. One thing I would do to increase straight talk on our team would be for us to _____
   _____
   _____

CHAPTER 4

Finding Your Authentic Self

I love the man who can smile in trouble, gather strength from distress and grow brave by reflection.

—THOMAS PAINE

HERE IS a quick exercise for you: make a list of the people you most enjoy being around. I mean, if you had half a day free and you could do anything, these are the people you would go see or invite to join you in your activities. Do you have your list? Now, look at the names you have written down. I am guessing it is a short list, and I would also wager a guess that each person on your list is someone you would label as "real," "genuine," or "authentic." At least that's the way my list came out. The people we want to be around by choice are the people who are who they are and let you be who you are, all while making you feel good about life.

What Is Authentic, and Why Does Remarkable Require It?

One of my favorite definitions of authenticity was offered by author and speaker Dr. Lance Secretan when he said, "Authenticity is the alignment of head, mouth, heart, and feet—thinking, saying, feeling, and doing the same thing—consistently. This builds trust, and followers love leaders they can trust." This alignment is really about comparing how I see me versus how others see me. Am I the same person in both cases? Or am I viewed totally different by those who know me versus how I see myself?

When we consider building a strong foundation layer in our Model for Remarkable, we must take into account how others view and are influenced by you. Your role as a leader who can consistently lead a team to remarkable performances hinges heavily on your ability to earn the trust of your team. And earning trust hinges heavily on your ability to be real and authentic. No one wants to be led or influenced by someone who is considered two-faced or fake. Being the real you—a real person—inspires others.

Authentic people are very clear on what their weaknesses are, as well as their strengths. They don't put on a show trying to make everyone think they have the answer all the time. IBM, since its very earliest days, has instilled a need for leaders to be authentic and real with their teams. The company does this by requiring every leader to embrace fact-based discussions and straight talk. One of our most senior leaders is known for reminding those he communicates with that they are entitled to their own opinion, but they cannot make up their own facts. His point is that the facts are the facts, good or bad, and we must own them so we can have candid conversations and make critical decisions about how to go forward. There is really no tolerance for those who insist that they have all the answers without involving their direct reports in the process of setting and executing the plan. IBM is a very competitive environment with a lot of really smart and talented people. Unfortunately, being smart and talented does not always lead to remarkable. When leaders begin to view themselves as the smartest people in the room, they have stepped onto the slippery slope of average and declining performance. Authentic leaders can have a very strong point of view about how things should be done, but they never assume it is the only way or even the best way. They leave the door open for members of their team to bring another point of view.

In my role enabling leaders at IBM, I always encourage leaders to embrace the thoughts and opinions of their teammates by saying the following: "This is what I think, but I am not the smartest one in the room... what do you think?" A leader who does this will put others at ease and open the door for communication that will always solve the problem. I once worked for a leader who did this, and even though he *was* the smartest person in the room most of the time, he never let himself think that he was. His authenticity gave him a real comfort in allowing others a shot at the solution. It also increased engagement of the team in everything we did. You were *expected* to have a point of view when you came to a meeting or a conference call with this leader. This raised the game of every member of the team and increased our chances of delivering a remarkable performance.

Developing Your Authentic Self

Author and television host Dr. Phil says, "Your authentic self is who you are when you have no fear of judgment, or before the world starts pushing you around and telling you who you're supposed to be. Your fictional self is who you are when you have a social mask on to please everyone else. Give yourself permission to be your authentic self." I find his choice of words interesting, "give yourself permission."

This "giving yourself permission" is more about revealing your authentic self than it is about developing some new character quality. In order to give yourself permission to be the real you in front of others and resist the temptation to put on a mask, it is helpful to have a clear understanding of what drives you. Authentic leaders must *be values driven*—this means having a clear vision of what you stand for and to whom you are accountable. In today's world it is easy to develop circumstantial values where the personal values you display are driven by the circumstances you find yourself in. Authentic people know who they are and exhibit the same values in every situation. From the earliest days of IBM, under the leadership of Thomas Watson and Thomas Watson, Jr., the focus on values and personal beliefs has been a strong determinant of what the company is about. Still, today you can hear leaders in the halls of IBM buildings worldwide explaining that they are doing something because it is in keeping with the core values of our company. Being true to who you are is not just a personal characteristic, but a characteristic of remarkable companies as well.

IBM is so committed to being a values-driven company that in July 2003 the CEO hosted a "Values Jam"¹ where tens of thousands of IBM employees could come together online to discuss and decide the values that would drive our company. It was during this 72-hour period that IBMers, working together (see the sidebar "What Is Jamming?"), decided that we would be guided by the following values:

1. Dedication to every client's success
2. Innovation that matters, for our company and for the world
3. Trust and personal responsibility in all relationships

Don't be fooled by the simplicity of these statements. They are at the center of everything we do and stand for at IBM. Leaders must develop their personal authenticity to operate within the boundaries of these values. When they do, they engage and motivate themselves and their teams. It is when this happens that remarkable performances are born.

Authentic leaders must also *be self-aware*—do your words match your actions? Become aware of how your thoughts, words, and actions line up in every situation you face and make note of what changes need to occur in either your thinking or your speaking to bring total alignment. Being self-aware is also about being cognizant of how your words and actions impact others. Self-aware leaders recognize their ability to affect others, positively or negatively, and then make adjustments to their communication style to get the maximum result. I have seen leaders win over the hearts and minds of their followers simply by acknowledging the effect they know they can have on others. One leader I worked with would say, "I know I can be like a bull in a china shop sometimes, so let me pause here and ask each of you to comment on the direction we should take with this project." You could see the tension in the room being reduced as people once again felt safe in opening up and sharing their point of view. That's being self-aware. Truly authentic leaders do not waste even a minute of your time trying to make you think they are something else. This builds trust among our team and opens the doors wide for improving performance and moving toward remarkable outcomes.

WHAT IS JAMMING?[2]

In 2001, IBM developed a collaborative technology that was soon to become known as Jam technology. This innovative approach to bringing groups of people together to discuss key issues has become a popular way to crowdsource new ideas. IBM specifically uses this technology to open a global dialogue around a very focused and specific topic. The online collaboration space provides a list of forums where you may enter your comments and follow the threaded discussion of other contributors worldwide. There are some scheduled "live chat" times, but the majority of the discussion is done whenever is most convenient for the contributor. A Jam usually lasts three days, giving everyone time to participate in the event.

After the Jam is concluded, IBM takes the inputs and, using IBM data analytic technology, develops the key themes into a findings white paper that is then shared with all the participants. IBM Jam events have been responsible for many key strategies with IBM and have even been applied to solving issues that face our planet.

Some Jam events over the years have addressed:

- Issues facing governments—Global Pulse—155 countries participated.
- Economic forum—1,600 experts participated.
- Smarter Planet discussion—2,000 students from 40 countries participated.
- Innovation Jam—1,000 companies participated.

Being Respected versus Being Liked

Authentic leaders have another characteristic that can be a tough one to master unless you are very comfortable with who you really are. People who are authentic put more value on *being respected versus being liked.* Many people tend to lean toward being liked versus being respected. An example of this is the leader who invests time in being well read

U.B.U.

I never cease to be amazed in my coaching business how often people are derailed by the opinions of others. Hardly a week goes by when people don't ask me how they should act when some person in their life does or says certain things to them. My answer is three little letters, *U.B.U.*, meaning "you be you." Here is what I encourage them to do:

1. Be yourself. Just because people are offering their opinions, regardless of how forcefully they do it, that does not really affect you or who you are. Everyone has an opinion, and most people feel the freedom to share their opinion.
2. Allow others to be themselves. Part of "you being you" is allowing other people to be themselves. If others being themselves means that they feel the need to freely distribute their opinions, then so be it.
3. Don't own someone else's opinions. Most opinions are exactly that, opinions. I do recommend listening, evaluating the other person's comments for validity, and then applying what is of value and letting the rest of it go.

and conversant on the subjects his or her team is dealing with. If you combine this with an open and direct communication style about these subjects, you find yourself respecting the fact that this high-level leader came prepared and with a point of view. When leaders do this, they do not have to submit to the point of view of others because they have taken the time to have their own thoughts. This approach allows the leaders to be open to other people's ideas and engage in a hardy debate about the choices available to the team. Leaders who are authentic are more interested in being respected for the value they bring to each and every exchange than for being liked for just going along with what everyone else thinks. Shakespeare said it best, "To thine own self be true."

Authentic leaders have no problem *being real*. By "real" I mean they put forward to others who they are without all the embellishment that less real people like to add to make their story seem more popular. Real people embrace their weaknesses and use them as doors to invite others into the conversation. As I mentioned earlier about an authentic leader being willing to invite other points of view to the team discussions, this can often be accomplished by telling a story where the leader made a mistake and how he or she needed the team's help to not do that again.

WHAT MAKES YOU GREAT

I had just come off the stage in Copenhagen, Denmark, after giving a speech to a large group of Nordic first-line managers when a man approached me.

"You want to know what makes you great in front of the audience?" he asked me.

"I would love to know the answer to that!" I said back to him.

He then commented, "You often speak about your weakness or your mistakes, and you tell us how you learned to do this thing or that thing. You never tell us about how great you are and how you always do the thing right that you are talking to us about."

He continued, "This is a very interesting approach, especially coming from an American."

As I thanked him for his kind compliment, I thought about how easy it was to earn his trust and respect just by being real, by being honest. His perception of Americans was that we come to his country and beat our chest and tell people how they should do things the way we do them, inferring that we always do things right the first time. The simple act of admitting struggle and setback had opened his ears to *want* to hear what I was saying. It opened an opportunity for me to increase my influence with him and the rest of the audience.

What makes you great and opens the door to remarkable performance is not touting where you are in life, but sharing openly how you got to where you are in life—no matter how ugly the path to get there may have been.

When strong leaders and executives in the organization do this sort of thing, their candor will help take down the walls that might keep the team from contributing to the solution.

There is a quiet humility surrounding authentic leaders. They know who they are and what they stand for, and they are comfortable letting other people have a say in the direction of the team. These authentic leaders do not have a need to overpower others or use their positional power to have their own way. They know what they believe, but they are comfortable inviting other points of view.

Is This Authentic Leadership?

I am often discouraged by how some leaders talk to their subordinates. What discourages me is how much profanity is used by these leaders to make their point with their people. Many times these subordinates then turn around and speak to their teams in the same way, and the pattern continues. I don't know how or when this habit of using foul language to speak to your subordinates became an acceptable leadership practice. In fact, I am sure it is not an *acceptable* leadership practice.

A recent *Wall Street Journal* article titled "A Curse Upon Your Career"[3] stated: "Generally, cursing at work can damn your career. Managers who cuss appear unprofessional and out of control, executive coaches and recruiters say. But that's not always the case. Deployed at the right moment and in the right setting, a well-chosen curse word can motivate a team, dissolve tension or win over an audience." The article went on to say, "'Companies increasingly prefer authentic leaders,' says Jeffrey Cohn, a CEO succession-planning expert. 'Using colorful language can play to your advantage—as long as you also demonstrate empathy and good business judgment.'"

Is this now the new definition of *authentic leadership*? I curse and use "colorful" language so that you think I am one of the boys (or girls as the article points out) and that makes you think I am real? I have another idea: you hold yourself to a higher standard and lead yourself in a way that makes me *want* to follow you because of the *person* you are. Any half-wit can throw around bad words and stomp his feet to get the attention of his people. Only truly inspirational leaders can exercise the control that is required to show respect to their people and others who may be watching or listening in.

Followers want to follow leaders who are consistent in their display of emotions and consistent in their responses to the various situations that present themselves each day. No one wants to follow or is inspired by leaders who erupt when situations change. Remarkable leaders who desire remarkable performance from each individual on their team must resist the impulse to blast away in the name of authenticity. If your authenticity shows disrespect for the people who work with you, then you are undermining any chance you have at remarkable.

It's a Trap

Don't fall for this trap of being like others and lowering your standards to appeal to the masses. As I mentioned earlier, if you establish a values-driven environment, falling into this trap of disrespecting your team becomes much more difficult. Even in a remarkable culture like IBM, we have explosions of bad behavior. It is how we handle them that allows us to channel them into positive actions. For example, I have rarely seen a demonstration of bad behavior without the leader coming back to the group and making things right. The value of personal responsibility doesn't mean you don't make mistakes; it means you own your mistakes and you do what you have to do to correct them. Remember, you are in leadership because you have been set apart from others to take others to a higher level. Being like everyone else and using your words to disrespect is not inspiring; it's disappointing, and remarkable performance will never flow from your team as you hope and expect it to flow.

CHAPTER 4 POWER POINTS

The focus of this chapter has been on how authentic people make the kind of leaders that can consistently lead a team into remarkable performances:

- **Be authentic.** Followers love to follow leaders they can trust, and trust is built by being you, not by trying to make people think you are something you are not.

Leader's Conversation Starter

To understand the level of authenticity your team feels, ask each member of the team to answer the following questions. Have the individual team members share their thoughts with the team.

When I think of our team, I feel compelled to:

a. Share my defeats as well as my victories with our team.

True _____ False _____ Why? _____

b. Ask others on our team what they think or feel about the current situation.

True _____ False _____ Why? _____

c. Always be prepared with my point of view of the current situation.

True _____ False _____ Why? _____

CHAPTER 5

I Didn't Intend for That to Happen

Direction, not intention determines your destination.
—ANDY STANLEY

THERE IS a television show that has been airing in the United States for over 20 years called *America's Funniest Home Videos*. The popularity of this reality television show is driven by what I call the "I can't believe that happened" dynamic. The show, if you are not familiar with it, features home videos sent in by people all across America. The premise is actually based on a Japanese television show, making this a global phenomenon—which really proves my point. Week after week, the show airs videos of people doing things that make you just shake your head and say, "Shouldn't that person have known better than to do that?" Whether it is some guy on a pogo stick who is on the roof of his house and is attempting to hit the swimming pool below, or the girl on the skateboard trying to navigate a stone stairway, it always ends up in pain for the participant. Shouldn't that person have known better than to do that? While these people may not have *intended* for their actions to land them on a television show as an example of what *not* to do, that is in fact the direction they were heading. Direction determines destination every time.

As part of the coaching work I do, it never ceases to amaze me how often I hear the words, "I didn't intend for that to happen." If I were completely honest, I would have to admit that I can recall saying those words myself years ago. The question that begs to be asked about a comment like that is, "If you did not intend for that outcome, then how did you get here?" There is only one answer to that question (and very few people get it right), and that is, because that's the direction you were going. Nothing can undermine the construction of your foundation layer in the Model for Remarkable faster than to find yourself on a path to a destination you did not intend.

The Principle of the Path

In his excellent book titled *The Principle of the Path: How to Get from Where You Are to Where You Want to Be,*[1] pastor and author Andy Stanley captures one of the greatest truths of life. It is one of those truths that when you read it and think about it for a couple of seconds, you overwhelmingly agree. However, when you are in the rush of life and in the process of trying to accomplish things in your life, it seems to be the furthest thing from your mind. There is a reason he labeled it a *principle* and not a concept or a suggestion. It is a principle (*law* might be a better word) because it is at work in your life every second of every day, whether you acknowledge that fact or not. Don't you think you would want to be aware of something with that much power over where you are going to end up?

The principle of the path goes like this: "Direction, not intention, determines your destination." The essence of this principle, as I just mentioned, is incredibly obvious, but it is incredibly elusive to most people; the choices you make determine the outcomes you experience. This has also been called the *law of cause and effect*: for every thought, choice, or action you take (the cause), there is an outcome (the effect). If you want a specific outcome, then you need to focus on the actions that drive that specific outcome. When my wife and I were teaching this principle to our children when they were young, we would point to the five-acre field next to our house, and I would ask, "Where are my green beans? I want to go pick some green beans!" My wife would then ask me if I planted any green beans or if I watered, weeded, and fertilized any green beans. I would tell her that I did not do any of that, to which she would respond, "Well, why then do you expect there to be green beans in that field?" It's a silly example, I know, and the children probably thought we were nuts, but the point is still a good one—why do we expect or even hope for an outcome (green beans) when we have not taken the necessary steps to generate that outcome?

Direction Is Everything

As we conclude Part I and our discussion of the importance of having a strong foundation for delivering remarkable performance, I want to leave you with one of the biggest obstacles to actually achieving remarkable. Andy Stanley says, "Direction is everything. Direction determines destination. That is why we cannot afford to live disconnected lives. We should break the habit of drawing a circle around individual decisions and events and dismissing them as isolated occurrences. These are steps; steps that lead somewhere, because life is connected." The biggest obstacle that many people face is that they do not connect their individual daily decisions to the outcomes they generate. All of us are currently on a path in every area of our lives. Think about your health for a moment. If you intend to lose 15 pounds, then there are certain dietary and exercise decisions you need to make every day if you hope to arrive at your intended destination. Think about your finances for a moment. If you intend to save $25,000 for a new car, then there are certain spending and saving decisions you need to make every day. What most of us do is say we intend to lose the weight or save the money, and then we do not stay on the path that leads in that direction. We somehow get off the intended path and onto another path that leads to a place we did not intend to go. Direction is everything!

Having a strong foundation for delivering remarkable performance is about having a clear definition of what you are trying to accomplish and connecting that with your values and why you want to accomplish it. The struggle that many average or mediocre performers face is in determining the exact path that leads to the desired outcome. Or they find the path but then don't remain on it when challenges arise. Distractions occur, choices are made, and paths are changed. It is almost imperceptible when it happens, and it can come with disastrous results.

The secret to fully experiencing the power of a strong foundation is not only being able to see the path to completion, but also recognizing when you need a course correction to return to the original path.

Defeating Detours

A few years ago it was considered a technological luxury if you had access to a GPS (global positioning system) in your car. Today, GPS technology is everywhere. It is standard equipment on most cars, and it is in our mobile phones and other handheld devices. When the technology was new and not widely available and I would run across it in a car I had just rented, I used it even if I really didn't need it—and I suspect this was true for a lot of people. I would type in all the info it asked for just so I could use it as backup for a trip I was pretty sure I could make without the GPS. It was cool and trendy, and I found it almost entertaining. However, today, with GPS technology everywhere, I find that I resist using the GPS because of all the effort required to enter the info the GPS needs to help me on a journey. I would almost just rather wing it on my journey. Plus I am a guy, and I don't really need help with directions.

Much like the GPS early days, when we start a new project or customer engagement, we naturally lay out our plan, and we have remarkable in our sights. But as time goes by and the challenges of day-to-day work increase, it is easy to lose our path and begin heading in a direction that will take us to a destination we did not intend. In order to defeat these detours that pop up along the path, remarkable performers take an intentional approach to navigating the path. All the remarkable performers I have met follow a set of specific steps to ensure they end up where they intend to end up.

The first and most important step is to have a *clearly marked map* from where you are to where you want to go. There is a button on my GPS that will show me the step-by-step instructions to my destination, or it will show me a map picture leading to my destination. Either way is fine, but one is needed. Most people who miss remarkable had the first and second steps mapped out, but that was about it. They think that getting started is the most important part, and they don't look much past that. Knowing all the steps, as well as you can know them, is necessary to advance in the direction of remarkable. Will things change? Almost certainly. Will you need to make changes to your plan? Almost certainly. But if you do not have a map with the course laid out, you will never be able to tell if you are on or off course.

Working with salespeople at IBM has really opened my eyes to the importance of having a plan. The problem is that most salespeople do not see the importance of thinking through their territory or account set, nor do they want to take the time to do it. That's why we teach a formal process for all sellers that forces them to think through the coming quarter and define in as much detail as possible how they will achieve their numbers. For example, when salespeople are assigned a territory, they are required to map it out and determine where the possible sales will come from. Whether they are managing 1 or 2 key accounts or covering 45 to 50 small and medium accounts, it is important to analyze the territory for potential opportunity. Some of the criteria they will use to do this analysis are things like:

- **The potential clients' industry affiliation.** What solutions might be possible that are based on the potential clients' industry affiliation?
- **The type of business the potential clients are in within this industry.** What solutions might be possible that are based on the type of business the potential clients are in within this industry?
- **Past products and solutions used by potential clients.** What types of products and solutions have these companies bought in the past?
- **The current economic conditions in this part of the world (United States, Europe, Asia, etc.).** What types of concerns or interests will these potential clients likely have that are based on current economic conditions in this geographic area?

The bottom line for all sellers is that they must have a coherent plan in place in order to focus their efforts in their assigned territory. We encourage every seller to be able to answer the question, "When you take into consideration this industry, in this geographic area, in this economy, what should this company be most concerned about over the next 12 to 18 months; and how can I help the company achieve its goals."

The second step that remarkable performers take is to *look for evidence* along the way that they are on the path to the desired destina-

WHEN LEADERS LOSE THE PATH

At IBM, leaders are taught that the attitudes and behaviors they display are directly related to their ability to remain on the path to their desired destination. We do this through the simple process of weekly progress reviews—progress against your metrics and progress with your people. This happens at all levels throughout the organization, and it allows the leaders to review their weekly progress with their leaders. There is a temptation for this to become merely a metrics review, but the remarkable leaders use this time first for understanding how their people are leading and then for coaching to improve attitude and behavior. The bottom line is that there needs to be trust between the leaders and their teams. When there is an erosion of trust, it generally occurs over time and is usually not due to some dramatic integrity issue. Here are the most common reasons:

1. The leader is not consistent in his or her response to changing circumstances. When followers are not sure if you will explode or implode on the reporting of news, they will generally stop reporting the news.

2. The leader does not communicate clearly what the expectations are and how we are doing against those expectations. Followers thrive on feedback. When they do not receive feedback, they begin to believe that what they do does not matter.

3. The leader seems to have all the answers and never asks for input from the team. If you do not include the members of your team in developing the plan, they will more than likely leave the execution of the plan up to you as well.

tion. Much like road signs along the highway, remarkable performers look for signs that the course they have chosen is the right one. These might be milestones or checkpoints along the journey. Each project or customer engagement will have a different set of milestones that tell you that you are going in the right direction. Average performers, like inattentive drivers who fail to watch the highway signage, have no idea when they have left the course they intended to take.

A third important step that remarkable performers take to ensure they reach their desired remarkable destination is to *ask for verification*. I joked earlier about being a guy and not needing help with directions. But as my wife will tell you, this is no laughing matter. Remarkable performers validate and verify with their customer or audience if they are on the right path. My wife has no problem asking people along our journey if this is the right road or the best road to get to where we want to go. Why is that so difficult for me? Because I like to think I have it all figured out. I know all the answers, and if I don't know the answer, I will fake it till I make it. This is *not* the path of remarkable performers. At IBM, we consistently work with our sales leaders on validating the progress of each sales deal with the customer. While we appreciate the salesperson's point of view, we establish a much higher level of trust in the evaluation when it has customer concurrence. Remarkable performers validate and verify what they think to be true, and they always do so from the customer's point of view.

The fourth and final step is a difficult one for many average performers, and that is to *make a course correction* when it is called for. The only thing worse than being off course is to be off course and not be willing to make the necessary corrections to get back on course. The most common cause for this is a leader not listening to or not wanting to hear from those on their team that changes need to be made. In the Introduction to this book, I recounted an anecdote about the warship *Vasa* and how the shipbuilders did not tell the king (the leader) that there was a problem with the construction. This happens all too often when the people closest to the action fear telling the leader about necessary corrections that need to be made. Part of IBM's culture includes a weekly assessment of progress against monthly and quarterly goals.

With each review an action plan is established to provide any needed course corrections. Unexpected "surprises" at the end of the quarter are not the way that teams turn in remarkable performances. Remarkable performances are recorded by teams with open, honest communication about the reality of the current circumstances and how that reality will relate to the desired final outcome. In the case of the *Vasa,* it was disastrous.

CHAPTER 5 POWER POINTS

Remarkable performances are a consistent by-product of teams that know the path to their destination and know how to stay on that path. In this chapter we looked at a major obstacle of individuals and teams desiring to establish a strong foundation for remarkable—maintaining the proper direction to get to their desired destination. Individuals and teams that achieve remarkable performance:

- Establish a clear path from where they are to where they want to be
- Look for evidence they are going in the right direction
- Ask for verification and validation of being on the right path
- Make course corrections when needed

Leader's Conversation Starter

If you want to guarantee that you are on the path that leads to your desired destination, then you need to ensure that your team is working in that direction as well. To do this, I recommend working through the following conversation starters to increase your chances of remarkable results. You can use these conversation starters as a project review for a project recently completed or as a project preview for a current or upcoming project.

1. What is the outcome that we are trying to accomplish? What will make that outcome remarkable in the customer's eyes?_____

_____

_____

_____

2. For the project in question, what are three "road signs" (success indicators) along the way that will tell us that we are proceeding in the correct direction for our desired outcome?_____

_____

_____

_____

3. Who can provide an outside point of view of our progress to validate and verify we are moving in the right direction?_____

_____

_____

_____

PART II

The Framework for Remarkable

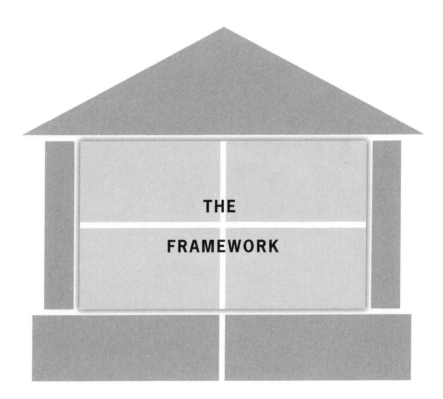

THE

FRAMEWORK

CHAPTER 6

The Model for Remarkable—the Framework That Makes Remarkable Work

Today I will do what others won't, so tomorrow
I can accomplish what others can't.

—JERRY RICE

WHEN YOU look at the history of the IBM Corporation, it is almost inconceivable how it became the remarkable company it is today in a highly competitive technology marketplace. From the unlikely alliance of a tabulating machine company, a time recording company, and a scale company comes one of the greatest computer companies in the world. How can that happen?

First, as we have discussed in Part I, there was a strong foundation to build upon. When Thomas Watson, Sr., came on board in 1914, he recognized the solid foundation and immediately began developing a framework for what would one day become the IBM Corporation, a global computing and technology powerhouse. The framework that Mr. Watson put into place would position the Computing-Tabulating-Recording Company (CTR) on a path to provide large-scale computing solutions for businesses in the United States and around the globe. He would leave the small office products business that CTR was originally involved with to others. This new direction began to pay off almost immediately, with revenue more than doubling in Watson's first four years. The new framework he had put in place would also pay off in remarkable ways as the United States and the world entered the computer age.

Constructing Remarkable

Now that we have a strong foundation to build upon consisting of the *what* and *why*, we can begin to construct our framework to house the important elements for consistently delivering remarkable performances—which will show us the *how*. The framework is the part of the building you interact with on a daily basis. It's what you see as you go about your day. It's out in the open.

The framework in our metaphor (see Figure 6.1) will be focused on the main traits that drive the actions we can observe. We will detail the four essential traits—also building blocks—that drive the actions

FIGURE 6.1 ■ **The Framework for Remarkable Performances**

of remarkable performers. We will thus learn how to put our goal into action.

Framework Building Block #1: Be Exceptional

When you build a house, if you don't do it right the first time, you undoubtedly will have to fix it later. That is why *be exceptional* is the first building block in our framework of remarkable.

If you have ever spent any time watching home fix-it shows on television in the United States and Canada over the past couple of years, you probably know the name *Mike Holmes*. Mike has a television show cleverly called *Holmes on Homes*. Mike and his team of experts come into the homes of average folks like you and me and fix problems caused by other building contractors previously hired. It sounds ironic, doesn't it: a home fix-it show where the goal is to fix other people's botched fixes? Is it just me, or is it alarming that you can have a top-rated television show if you will just fix things that should have already been fixed, if only the people fixing them had done the right thing?

If you watch the show for more than 10 minutes, you learn that Mike Holmes is a guy who genuinely cares about the people he is helping, and their homes. He has made a name for himself—and caused others to take notice—by doing truly exceptional work. His personal motto, as well as his website name and the tattoo on his arm, is "Make It Right," and that is exactly what he does, episode after episode. Often the project that he is there to fix has already cost the homeowners tens of thousands of dollars and sometimes has even resulted in physical injury. What I like about Mike Holmes is that he is what I imagine a true craftsman to be. He cares about his work, he cares about his customers, and he will settle for nothing less than the very best. He would never cut a corner, and he would never leave something undone that could and should be done. He is often called a hero by those he does work for because he is fixing very bad problems in their lives, and most times he is paying the bill to do it. But as Mike says, "I don't think of myself as a hero; I think of myself as a contractor." Like I said, he is a good guy just trying to right a wrong in an exceptional way.

WRECKING BALL TO BEING EXCEPTIONAL:
A LACK OF PRIDE IN ONE'S WORK

A wrecking ball to being exceptional can be found in the *lack of pride some people take in their work*. Regardless of whether or not there is a building code or a building inspector coming to review your work, become a remarkable performer and do it right because it is a reflection of you. State, "I stand behind it; I put my name on it."

Steve Jobs at Apple Computer had the people who built the Macintosh computer sign the inside cover. When the design team members reminded him that the covers on a Mac are locked and no one will ever see the names, he told them that an artist always signs his work. Would you put your name on the work that you do?

Actually, it already has your name on it whether you put it there boldly or not; that's why you do it right whether someone is watching over your shoulder or not. Every one of the contractors who did the work that Mike Holmes had to fix had their names on those jobs. Mike Holmes is too nice to use their names on the television show, but they know who they are, and so do the homeowners in the area where the work was done. I wonder if those faulty contractors ever watch the show. I think they should be forced to watch it as part of their retraining efforts.

Just like Mike Holmes, the IBM Corporation decided early to "make it right." Being exceptional is a core belief inside the framework that makes up IBM. From the earliest days of the company's founding, Thomas Watson, Sr., and Thomas Watson, Jr., made customer service the focal point of everything the company did. The products that were developed and the service that was provided were all put in place with the idea that an exceptional experience would be how a customer would define what working with IBM was all about.

Building remarkable means that you don't cut corners or take the easy path to save time or costs. You do it right because that is what remarkable people do. You do exceptional work.

Framework Building Block #2: Be Prepared

If you are not prepared to build a house, you will get nowhere in the process. This is why the second building block in our framework is *be prepared.*

In Mike Holmes's world, being prepared means knowing his craft. Mike and his team of experts have prepared by acquiring the necessary skills through study, apprenticeship, and experience. Like Mike, you should always be preparing. To prepare, I like to read and stay up-to-date on the areas of my interests. A friend asked me why I made reading such a priority. I told him I was preparing. He asked me what I was preparing for. I said I didn't know, but when the opportunity presented itself, I wanted to be ready. If you are waiting for the opportunity to present itself before getting prepared, you could miss the opportunity altogether.

A key component of the ongoing training of an IBM salesperson or sales manager is showing them how to get, and stay, prepared. To do this, every seller is instructed in the use of both internal IBM resources and external research tools to be more prepared to serve our clients. More recently we have begun working with our sellers and leaders on the use of social media tools like Twitter, LinkedIn, and Facebook to stay up-to-date and ready in today's fast-paced and rapidly changing world. One simple yet effective way to stay current and prepared is to set up your Twitter account to "listen" to (receive tweets from) the identified experts in your field of interest. For example, if you are selling predictive analytic solutions, then you need to determine who are the thought leaders in the predictive analytic area, who are the customers using predictive analytics, and which industry groups are most interested in predictive analytics. Then use Twitter to follow those people and groups. I also recommend to our sellers that they establish Google Alerts to search the Internet for keywords or customer names and bring those results directly to the sellers' inboxes.

Most sellers instantly reject a lot of the social media tools today for fear that they are too time consuming and don't provide any specific value. My view is a bit different. You do not have the time to search the

Internet for the nuggets of information that could help you be more prepared and more credible with your clients. If you use these social technologies correctly, however, they will do the searching for you and bring the results to your inbox each morning. I call it "15 minutes and a cup of coffee." Set your tools up to do the work, and then you review the results daily over your morning coffee. It seems simple, but it can be a difference maker.

Do you take time each week to improve your skills or your knowledge in the area of your interests? Having the right skills got you where you are today, but those skills are not sufficient to prepare you for where you must be tomorrow. Sorry, but what you brought to *the game* yesterday kept you in *the game* yesterday, but it's not enough to keep you on the roster today, much less tomorrow! Even if you were remarkable in getting to where you are, it will not be enough to keep you remarkable in the future. What was remarkable yesterday is merely good enough today.

WRECKING BALL TO BEING PREPARED: MISSING OPPORTUNITIES TO LEARN

Another wrecking ball to remarkable performances that can sneak up on even the best of us is not taking every opportunity presented to us to increase our skills and abilities. To protect yourself from this wrecking ball, you should always be learning. When you look closely at how remarkable performers function, you begin to notice that they are not only concerned with the performance itself; they are also concerned with being the very best they can be. Remarkable performers focus on doing their best as their top priority, knowing that by doing so, the performance will take care of itself. How do remarkable performers do their best? They continually practice improvement and learning. They focus less on *proving* their value, and rather they use energy *improving* their value. They do this by reading, studying the work of others, and trying new things in their areas of expertise that will help them expand their borders and enlarge their capabilities.

Never stop learning and growing; continuing to expand your knowledge and experience is a sign of a remarkable person.

A Remarkable-Me Moment

In Figure 6.2, take a moment to document actions you could take to increase your learning potential in the area of your expertise. Draw a line from the circles representing learning modes to the rectangles on the left and write a couple of action steps to get you moving in the right direction. For example, you could draw a line from "Audiobooks" to a

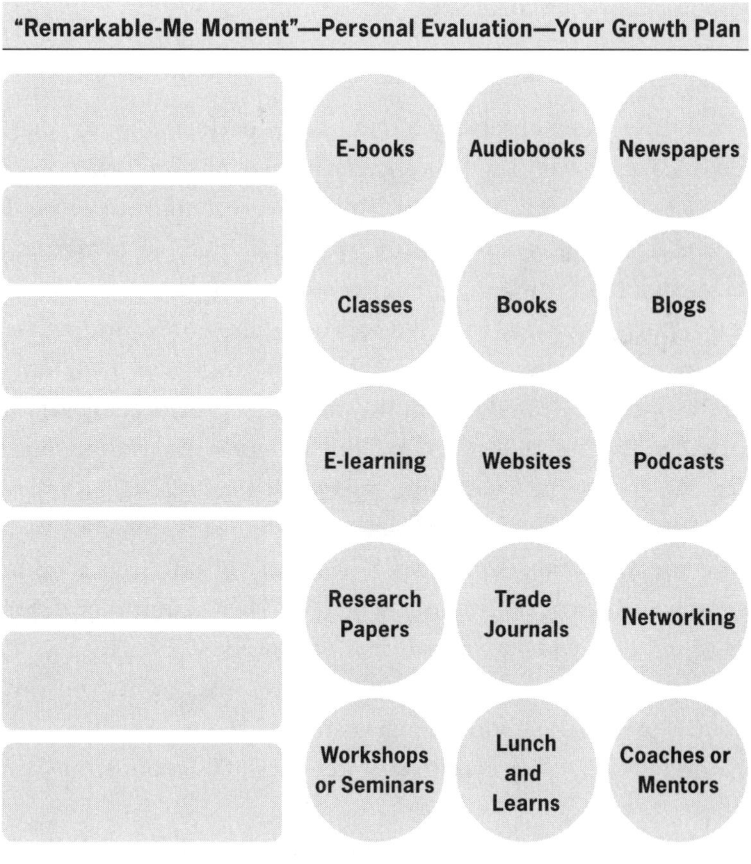

"Remarkable-Me Moment"—Personal Evaluation—Your Growth Plan

	E-books	Audiobooks	Newspapers
	Classes	Books	Blogs
	E-learning	Websites	Podcasts
	Research Papers	Trade Journals	Networking
	Workshops or Seminars	Lunch and Learns	Coaches or Mentors

FIGURE 6.2 ▪ Your Personal Growth Plan

rectangle and make the note, "Subscribe to an audiobook website and search for applicable titles."

Framework Building Block #3: Be Disciplined

It's one thing to be prepared and to do exceptional work. If you want to repeat remarkable, however, you also need to *be disciplined*—which becomes the third building block in our framework.

What does it mean to be disciplined? In his terrific book *The Compound Effect,*[1] author and *Success Magazine* editor Darren Hardy presents a principle that is essential to all success. It is incredibly important that when you make the commitment to remarkable performances, you embrace this core principle:

Small, smart choices + consistency + time = radical difference

It is so easy when observing a remarkable performance to label the person or company as gifted, lucky, advantaged, or some other descriptor that lets us off the hook for delivering remarkable ourselves. The truth is that we all have the ability for remarkable performance, but not all people, nor all companies, are willing to do the small, seemingly insignificant things that, if done consistently over time, create an environment where remarkable becomes a way of life. For example, at IBM, one of the seemingly insignificant things provided to every person in the organization is an enormous (and growing) online training library. We call this the Learning for Growth system, and it provides hundreds and hundreds of web-based audio and video content that covers every area that IBM serves. The library of offerings is updated frequently and is a great resource whenever IBM acquires or develops a new solution. If you have a customer who needs a particular solution that you may not be as well versed in as you need to be, you simply log on and search the library. Each year, IBM senior executive use the Learning for Growth system to post key messages about strategy and direction.

My friends from other companies are amazed that IBM would make such a financial commitment to our personal growth and development. Of course, having a resource like this and using it are two totally separate things. This is where discipline comes in. We live in a quick-fix, silver bullet kind of a world where everyone wants to know the fastest way to have more money, lose more weight, and have more success. In financial success as well as weight loss success, there are no silver bullets, and there is no substitute for making the small, smart choices that will lead to our success. In fact, most times the choices are so small and seemingly insignificant that they don't even seem like choices.

Mr. Hardy emphasizes the value of the basics of being disciplined: make good decisions, develop positive habits, and be consistent over time. These elements build momentum and ensure success. As the author says, "Your only path to success is through a continuum of mundane, unsexy, unexciting, and sometimes difficult daily disciplines compounded over time." I believe the same when it comes to remark-able: I think that the only path to being truly remarkable in all that we do is *through a continuum of mundane, unsexy, unexciting, and sometimes difficult daily disciplines compounded over time.* The question we have to ask ourselves is whether we are compounding positive choices and habits or negative ones. We are definitely compounding something, but what is it?

Most people try to make good choices. I don't know a lot of people who ask, "What can I do today to screw up my life?" or even, "What can I do today to stay average?" Instead of intentionally making bad decisions and developing bad habits, most people sleepwalk through their choices, not really viewing them as choices but rather *defaults.* Who chooses how much you eat, sleep, or exercise? You do. Who chooses how you spend your time? You do. If and when you wish to make a change in your life, you can do it. But it requires that you make it a *conscious* choice to practice and drive positive habits until they compound into making you remarkable over time.

To ensure that you stay disciplined, track every action. Whether you are working on better money management or trying to lose weight, you need to start by becoming aware of the choices you are currently mak-ing. You need a *baseline* measure, a picture of where you spend your

WRECKING BALL TO BEING DISCIPLINED: MISMANAGING TIME

It is difficult to estimate how many people I have seen allow their superior skills go to waste by not having a disciplined approach to their life and work. Most people don't have a realistic measurement of where they spend their time, and in fact mismanage their time, which is a wrecking ball to being disciplined. For example, when I ask the people I coach why they don't read more, the answer is almost always, "I don't have enough time." And they continue to say this even when I tell them it is one of the most positive things they can do to increase their chances for success. Of course, when I quiz them on how they spent the previous day, I get an accounting that looks something like this:

- Slept later than I meant too
- Watched my favorite morning news show on TV
- Ran into bad traffic on the way to work, but listened to my new CD of [fill in the artist]
- Got to work on time, but just barely, actually a couple of minutes late
- Looked at my favorite social media sites on the computer
- Texted with several friends about what we were doing tonight
- Played the new [fill in the video game] when I got home
- Watched the evening news
- Watched *American Idol* and *NCIS*
- Stayed up late watching a really cool movie

I get tired just listening to why they can't find any time to read, the single biggest discipline I have found to positioning yourself for success. The answer they should have given me is, "I didn't *take* the time."

time and how you make decisions today. To do this, you need to track everything you do in the area you are trying to improve. If improving your budget, track every penny you spend for the next 30 days. If trying to lose weight, track everything you put in your mouth and every minute you exercise over the next 30 days. If trying to increase your potential for remarkable performances, track your preparation habits, your ability to focus, your dedication to the project, your tenacity and willingness to push through the challenges.

This process is not as precise as tracking dollars or calories, but you can use this method to take note of the way you are talking to yourself, the number and type of distractions that interrupted your work, and the kinds of things that made you want to quit and walk away. You can actually begin to track the number of times you are tempted to check your e-mail or Twitter. By tracking what you are doing, your eyes will be opened to what is really going on so that you can make corrections to your choices and develop new, more positive habits. After tracking the things mentioned above, you will be able to make intentional decisions about the environment where you work and the use of technology (where most of the distractions come from). You will be able to recognize early any frustrations that might lead you toward giving up. Tracking your thoughts may sound a bit like nailing Jell-O to a wall, but awareness is the key to moving intentionally toward being remarkable.

Good habits are as addictive as bad habits, and a lot more rewarding.
—HARVEY MACKAY

Tracking your behaviors and taking daily action in the area of setting goals are other habits that can make a big difference in your ability to compound positive results. Goals can be a tough area for a lot of people. Most solid performers have goals, but they struggle with writing them down and reviewing them frequently like the most remarkable people among us do. As a result of this exercise, you can begin writing and reviewing your goals. Darren Hardy writes, "Something almost magical happens when you organize and focus your creative power on a well-defined target."[2]

The vast majority of everything we think, feel, do, and achieve is a result of a learned habit. Our habits and routines allow us to use minimal conscious energy for everyday tasks. By tracking your actions, you can begin to see patterns or habits that you have learned over time. Identify the habits that you need to change, and begin today to establish a daily routine of good habits.

Discipline also means developing the habit of correcting things that were not done right the first time. Mike Holmes almost always has to tear things down in order to build them back correctly. He has never said, "We have to rip out the basement floor, and that is going to take a lot of time and effort; let's just cover it over with something that makes it look good." He makes it right by executing a disciplined approach to solving every problem he faces.

To be disciplined, you must also be consistent. This means you replicate the good habits you begin. Hardy uses the metaphor of a well pump to describe the effect that being consistent has on your overall success. If you have ever seen a hand pump for a well, you know that you must pump the handle for a couple of minutes before any water begins to flow. Once it is flowing, a slow and steady pumping continues to generate results. If you stop pumping for even a few seconds, the water falls back down the pipe into the well, and you have to start all over again.

This is really a big deal at IBM, and the repetitive motion of the well pump is an excellent metaphor for how it works for leaders at all levels. We train leaders to master a few significant metrics to manage their business. Weekly checkpoints in one-on-one and one-on-group discussions ensure that nothing is left to chance. We call this the weekly *sales cadence,* and it is used to make sure everyone is walking in the same direction and on the same page. In a typical weekly sales cadence, the first-line manager will review the current month and quarter opportunities that the salesperson is working on and look for areas to coach and assist the seller. The first-line manager then participates in a sales cadence with his or her manager to report progress and ask for help where needed. This process continues to the highest levels of the sales organization. The deal-by-deal details may diminish as the cadence goes higher in the organization, but the focus on progress against the metrics is understood throughout the organization. This consistency

around the metrics and progress helps to maintain the discipline necessary to drive remarkable performance.

The same is true with developing your remarkable mindset. Getting started is not really that hard; but when the remarkable results
you hope for do not come overnight, then you may stop—and whatever
progress you have made falls back into the well. This is really easy to
see when you are trying to lose weight, and after two weeks of hard
work and diligence you only lose two pounds. There is a bit of dis-
appointment, you grab a bag of chips, and the two weeks' work you
did just evaporated. You have to start pumping all over again. As you
pursue remarkable performance, you will notice that consistency has
a lot to do with rejecting the desire to cut corners and take a quick fix
even when you know that it will not solve the long-term problem. Just
like the Mike Holmes examples earlier, you have to do it right the first
time, or you end up average or worse.

Framework Building Block #4: Be Persistent

None of these traits will stick in repeating remarkable performances
if you don't make the conscious choice to *be persistent*—which is the
fourth building block in our framework. You can *never* be or lead
remarkable if you quit when things get difficult. Explorer Ed Stafford
walked the entire Amazon River. Did he ever think about quitting?
Yes. Did he ever talk about quitting? Yes. Did he ever quit? No. That's
persistence. Remarkable!

In order to be persistent, remarkable people choose to "fail forward" instead of quitting when failure or setbacks occur. Before we
talk about failing forward, let's explore failure in general. A common misperception exists about remarkable people and remarkable
performances. That misperception is that remarkable people are just
so good that they do not lose or have setbacks; everything just kind
of works for them. One thing is for sure: truly remarkable people
who lead truly remarkable performances do their homework, prepare themselves, and persist in such a way as to reduce the number
of setbacks and defeats. But reducing setbacks and defeats doesn't

WRECKING BALL TO BEING PERSISTENT: SKIPPING THE FOUNDATION

People generally love to start new things, but fewer people are there to finish them. The number one reason this happens is that when people start the tasks, they haven't laid the foundation. That is, they (1) have not clearly defined the outcome and (2) have not clearly cemented their why. Thus, when something else comes along, they become distracted. And that break in focus is the beginning of the end for their previous goal. Quitting can be habit forming. You will not find remarkable people who have a history of quitting. If you are doing the right things for the right reasons, then sticking to the task and performing it in a remarkable way will become a whole lot easier. Remarkable performances are led by remarkable people who realize early that things could get tough and distractions could appear. Remarkable people keep the what and the why in focus so they are not tempted to quit. So even though we are now working on the framework, I hope you can see how the foundation continues to be imperative in all you do.

mean eliminating them. That's an impossible dream. The difference between average performers and remarkable performers is how they see and use their setbacks and defeats. This is an incredibly important point for anyone desiring to lead a remarkable performance: you will always face opposition of some form—whether opposition to your ideas or your actions. This opposition may come from the environment where you are doing your work, or it may come from other people with whom you are trying to work. Opposition from people is often difficult to overcome because we have a hard time imagining that someone does not want to see us succeed. Nonremarkable people often take offense when remarkable people begin to do their thing. Why? Because nonremarkable people don't do what it takes to be remarkable, and thus remarkable people make them look bad. In other words, remarkable people raise the bar on performance while at the same time shining a spotlight on subpar or average performances.

Failure is an inside job. So is success. If you want to achieve, you have to win the war in your thinking first. You can't let the failure outside you get inside you.

—JOHN MAXWELL

The way remarkable performers overcome these setbacks and defeats is by developing the ability to *fail forward*—a concept that author and speaker John Maxwell discusses.[3] Failing forward involves viewing every setback or defeat as an opportunity to learn and grow. Average performers often become derailed by a defeat, but a remarkable performer will take the lesson from the defeat and apply it to the next attempt at the task. I used to tell my children, "Let's make all new mistakes today." I wanted them to know that making mistakes and having setbacks was not the problem. We all make mistakes. Repeating the same mistakes you committed yesterday—now that would be a problem.

The Track to Remarkable

As I have shared in discussing the foundation of our model for remarkable performances, being or leading remarkable does not just happen; it develops from taking an intentional approach to everything you do. You have to take action. However, sometimes it is difficult to determine exactly what actions to take. In order to develop a better understanding of exactly what you need to do to be on a path for remarkable performances, ensure the actions (choices) you take are *positively* compounding toward remarkable. As I've laid out in this chapter on the framework, the most important step you can take to begin doing things right the first time and compounding positive results is to construct your remarkable performance with the principles or building blocks that will serve as supporting walls.

The great lesson here for anyone desiring to lead or provide remarkable performances is that you have incredible power to *change your life by changing your choices*. If you want to grow and change, then you must make small, good choices that develop positive habits that you can do consistently over time—compounding into remarkable performances.

When we add the framework to our foundational building blocks, we now have the makings of our model for delivering and repeating remarkable performances (Figure 6.3).

IBM and the Model for Remarkable

Looking back over my years of service at IBM, I can see how each of these components of my Model for Remarkable has been in play. From

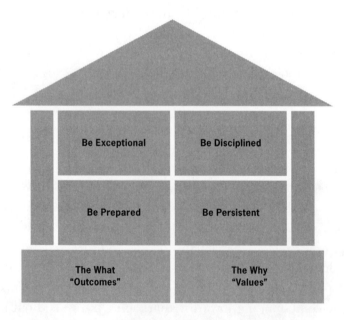

FIGURE 6.3 ▪ The Foundation and the Framework
of Our Model for Remarkable

my earliest years as a sales guy to these more recent years of enabling leaders, each of the four components has been present.

Be exceptional. IBM has always prided itself on hiring the best, but even after hiring what it considers to be the best, it sends everyone to school. In 1916, IBM founder Thomas Watson, Sr., established one of the first employee education departments. Mr. Watson believed that education and continual learning were key to every employee's, and thus IBM's, success. When I started, every new hire went away for weeks to a series of schools that would provide the foundation required to interact with customers and be credible about computer technology and how it can help customers to improve their business. Now entry training consists of online training components combined with classroom components to fully educate and test each new hire. This Global Sales School[4] approach is an innovative approach to learning by doing.

Be disciplined. The IBM way is to do the things that ensure success. It is not appropriate or acceptable to cut corners in any way. From the weekly sales cadence to the manager-employee one-on-one meetings, nothing is left to chance. If you desire a specific outcome, then you must take the disciplined set of steps to generate that outcome.

Be prepared. The worst thing you can do at IBM is show up to anything unprepared. There is absolutely no tolerance for people who are not ready and able to contribute. And *prepared* does not just mean knowing what is going on. Being prepared means having a point of view about what's going on. As I described earlier, IBM goes far beyond what the average company provides for employee education. Through the impressive Learning for Growth system, every IBM employee is handed the tools needed not only to be prepared but to be credible and relevant in the issues and solutions that will affect clients and prospects.

Be persistent. It is instilled from your very first day on the job that we never quit, we never give up—we are IBM!

CHAPTER 6 POWER POINTS

In this chapter we have introduced the framework for our Model for Remarkable. To review, here are the four building blocks we discussed:

1. Be exceptional.
2. Be prepared.
3. Be disciplined.
4. Be persistent.

Leader's Conversation Starters

As a leader desiring to lead remarkable performances, there are several areas I would want to review with my team. Take a few moments in your next team meeting to discuss these questions with your team:

1. How would you rate our team on a scale of 1 to 10, where 1 means "we don't do it" and 10 means "we do it all the time," on these statements:
   a. We do exceptional work. _____
   b. We have a disciplined approach to our work. _____
   c. We are always prepared. _____
   d. We never quit or give up. _____

2. What is the evidence that supports your ratings above?
   a. Exceptional: _____
   b. Disciplined: _____
   c. Prepared: _____
   d. Persistent: _____

3. What could we do to improve our team in these areas?
   a. Exceptional: _____
   b. Disciplined: _____
   c. Prepared: _____
   d. Persistent: _____

CHAPTER 7

Cruise Control

Success seems to be connected with action.
Successful people keep moving.

—CONRAD HILTON

NEVITABLY, EVERY year an e-mail gets passed around touting the
Stella Awards.[1] Supposedly, the Stella Awards are a collection of the
most frivolous lawsuits for the previous 12 months and are named after
the woman (Stella) who successfully sued McDonald's when she spilled
hot coffee on herself. Every year the "awards" take on a life of their
own with many bogus stories,[2] a number of which are repeated year
after year. The all-time leading bogus story (i.e., it wins every year) is
about a lawsuit supposedly filed by a man (or a woman depending on
the year) who bought a new 32-foot motor home, took it for a drive,
turned on the cruise control at 70 miles per hour, and then got out of
the driver's seat and went to the back of the motor home to make a cup
of coffee. Of course, the motor home crashed, and the driver sued the
manufacturer for not telling him (or her) that you could not do this.

It may be all bogus, but it reminds me of what I see so many times
when individuals and teams achieve remarkable performances. We are
tempted to turn on the cruise control and enjoy our success as we motor
along the roadway toward our next challenge. It appears to be a part of
our human nature to follow a remarkable performance with a period
of rest or a letdown. We are pleased with our performance, we develop
a pride around it, and then we place our task execution on cruise control as we move to the next project. In order to establish a strong and
enduring framework in our Model for Remarkable, we must avoid this
temptation to power up the cruise control. Much like the driver of the
motor home, we are headed for a crash when we allow this to happen.

While walking in an airport recently, I passed a young man wearing a T-shirt that proudly proclaimed, "It Just Happened." From the looks of this 20-something, the shirt was right! However, this is generally not the way things take place in real life. Life doesn't just "happen." Life is a series of choices, made either consciously or unconsciously. Most people really don't view life as a series of choices. We allow things to kind of happen to us and around us, and then we react or redirect based on the consequences of what happened. Remarkable performers live life differently. Remarkable performers have chosen (*chosen* being the operative word here) to go at life with a more intentional (another powerful word) approach. They decide where they want to end up and then make the proper choices to get there. Choices matter, and there are consequences to every choice, either positive or negative. Every choice takes me either closer to where I want to be or further away. As we discussed earlier, my choices determine the direction I am traveling, and my direction determines where I am going to end up.

A Higher Standard

I once gave a speech to a large group of sales professionals, and as I was wrapping up my comments and leaving the audience members with an encouraging word about developing their daily disciplines for success, one of them asked me to share my daily disciplines. When I finished sharing my disciplines with them, another person said, "You seem to expect way more of yourself than anyone else expects of you." I would have been fine with that, but then he continued, "Why are you so hard on yourself?"

High expectations are the key to everything.

—SAM WALTON

Later that day, as I boarded my plane and headed for home, I kept thinking about that comment and whether or not I was too hard on myself. What I know about me—and that the guy who asked the question does not know—is that if I did not challenge myself to a higher standard, I would easily fall into a complacent lifestyle. What I know about me is that the things I need to do to be successful and keep growing are *easy*; unfortunately, it is also really easy *not to do them*. I could get really comfortable with living an undisciplined life, but living an undisciplined life will compound over time, and what seems like a small concession today will be an enormous negative in my life five years from now. Author and speaker Jim Rohn liked to say, "It is dangerous to look at an undisciplined day and think that no harm has been done." Undisciplined days lead to undisciplined weeks, and so on and so on. Am I too hard on myself? Maybe, but I know what will happen if I don't do what I feel I need to.

Remarkable people do the things that other people are not willing to do. Remarkable people set the standard for their lives and their performances; they do not allow others to set the standard for them. Remarkable people know that growing and developing is hard work and that no one is going to hold their feet to the fire but them. Remarkable people keep the promises they make to themselves. That may sound easy enough, but I have found that I am the easiest person to deceive. I would love to tell myself that I can have that doughnut and that I don't need to run that mile, but I promised myself I would honor my decision to stay fit and healthy, and so I will. I read a Twitter tweet from leadership author and speaker Robin Sharma that said, "I got up to exercise this morning when I didn't want to because I promised myself I would." I love the thought of making and *keeping* promises to myself. "Making" is easy; "keeping" is another story. Many of us are not so good at doing this, but to be remarkable you must develop this characteristic.

IBM on Cruise Control and a Near Fatal Crash

As I mentioned earlier, the early 1990s were not good for IBM. I was working my way up through the sales organization and attempting to become a first-line sales manager when everything began coming apart. As in most cases of near business collapse, it did not happen

overnight. The slow and steady decline of market share had been building for years. But the cruise control had been set, and the driver had
gone to the kitchen for a coffee. Mainframe computers are what got
us here, and mainframe computers would take us where we wanted
to go. Unfortunately, the quickly evolving personal computer market
would have a few things to say about that. While the rest of the world
was moving toward the newer technologies, IBM was holding on to
what worked in the past. If we could just make mainframes faster and
cheaper, we would be okay.

With a change in leadership at IBM came a change in how the
company would move forward in the ever-changing computer technology field. There would be new standards of performance set and
a new accountability for getting things done. Similar to the business
downturn that occurred in the 1990s, the course correction did not
happen overnight. The slow and steady consistency of the new direction would prove to be an incredibly positive thing to do. The cruise
control was turned off, and the driver took control of where this business would go next.

Setting Standards and Keeping
Promises to Myself

College basketball coach Rick Pitino once said, "Set higher standards
for your own performance than anyone around you, and it won't matter
whether you have a tough boss or an easy one. It won't matter whether
the competition is pushing you hard, because you'll be competing with
yourself." This is what transpired at IBM to set it on a course to regain
remarkable company status. High standards were set for personal and
corporate performance. There was a push toward innovation and a
new way of thinking about the computer marketplace, our customers,
and ourselves. Nothing was sacred. Everything was up for evaluation.
We had to be better at what we did, and we had to keep the promises
we had made to our customers and to ourselves.

As someone desiring to deliver remarkable performances, you need
to develop the habit or discipline of setting your own standards for

performance and holding yourself accountable for the results. It is very easy to deceive ourselves into thinking we have done everything we could possibly do and that we did it to the highest level possible. As a 24-year, retired FBI agent specializing in counterintelligence, LaRae Quy wrote in her *Empower the Leader* blog,[3] "We've carefully packaged ourselves to look and act in a manner that ensures success in the world. Our ego has dressed us up for so long that many of us don't even know how to begin to peel back the layers of illusion to expose cold, hard facts about ourselves." Doesn't that just sound like us? Revealing the cold, hard facts about me has shown me that I need to turn off the cruise control and establish my own standards for performance. I need to hold my own feet to the fire, and I need to keep the promises I make to myself.

Look at Figure 7.1, and then take a few minutes to think through the standards that you feel would be important for your life. I have given you a couple of idea starters, but your situation may be unique, and you are the only person who can determine what the nonnegotiable standards should be for you. I would use an exercise like this

Time out of bed every day	When I feel like it
	At the last minute
How many books will you read this year?	Who's got time to read?
	Maybe a couple, as time permits

FIGURE 7.1 ■ **My Personal Standards**

with my IBM team to establish a mindset of personal responsibility. If each of us is not setting high standards for our own performance, then IBM as a whole will never reach the levels of remarkable performance that the company aspires to. I learned early with my team that we all needed to be moving toward remarkable if we ever hoped to reach it and repeat it as a team.

Some other examples of personal standards that you should consider are:

- **Relationships (horizontal).** By "horizontal" I mean peer-level relationships. Do you have people in your life who you can meet with each month, or each week, who are people just like you trying to grow and improve? If you give these trusted friends the permission to alert you to any blind spots you may have and to challenge you when they think your actions are not in keeping with your personal standards, you will establish something that all remarkable performers have—accountability.

- **Relationships (vertical).** By "vertical" I mean people you look up to who have traveled the path that you are trying to travel. You should consider these people to be your coaches or mentors. These are incredibly valuable relationships for helping you to see the big picture and check to ensure the direction in which you are heading leads to the destination you desire.

Vertical goes two directions, which means you should also play the coach and mentor to younger individuals who are pursuing their life aspirations. I was not sure I had a lot to share when I first started this practice, but I was surprised to learn that the struggles these young people were dealing with were incredibly similar to the struggles I had dealt with. Funny, huh? As I tell them when I meet with them, you don't have time to make all the same mistakes I made. Do yourself a favor and learn from me what *not* to do so you can spend your valuable time doing it right.

- **Saying no.** When you say yes to one thing, you have, by default, said no to something else. You should establish a standard in your life to be fully aware of exactly what you have just said no to when you made your "yes" choice. Saying no helps keep you centered and focused on the fact that all of life is a series of choices.

Always dream and shoot higher than you know you can do. Don't bother just to be better than your contemporaries or predecessors. Try to be better than yourself.
—WILLIAM FAULKNER

Having a higher standard for your life is an easy thing to do; it is also an easy thing *not* to do. Most people you meet are in a constant state of comparing themselves with others. It is easy to feel good about where I am in life and what I am accomplishing based on how I compare with my neighbor or my friend. College basketball coach John Wooden liked to tell his players, "Never try to be better than someone else. Learn from others, and try to be the best you can be. Success is the by-product of that preparation." Nothing against my neighbor or friend, but I can do more; I can do better than I did yesterday. If I want to really be considered a remarkable performer and a remarkable person, then I need to hold myself to a higher standard. I can't be distracted by other people thinking I am too hard on myself. Being better than yourself takes an intentional approach to life, but it pays enormous long-term dividends.

Seeing Yourself as You Really Are

A quotation by Anais Nin says, "We don't see things as they are, we see things as we are." I find great truth in this statement, especially when I am working with individuals or teams on improving their performance. Many people fail to take the necessary steps to improve themselves or their teams because they have a flawed view of their reality. They think they are better than they are, and they don't feel like any action is required to change things. This is how the cruise control gets set in your life; this is what leads to inferior performances.

This is what was going on with IBM in the 1990s. After so many years of growing revenue and market share, it was really easy to just keep doing what we were doing. Success can distract you that way. The market was changing all around us, and yet we kept doing what we were doing until it almost caused bankruptcy. The final wake-up call came when, after two years of losses in excess of $1 billion, IBM announced an $8 billion loss in 1992. It was the single largest one-year corporate loss in U.S. history. It's been said that nothing fails like success. Success breeds complacency if you allow it to do so. Once that happens, it is only a matter of time before performance will begin to wane.

Even if you just completed what would be considered a remarkable performance, this kind of "I have arrived," "I have been successful," thinking can set your cruise control in a manner that will keep you from repeating your remarkable ways. Seeing yourself as you really are is an important first step in making sure that the cruise control is never allowed to be set.

Once you come to grips with the "real you," you can begin the process of setting your personal standards for remarkable and setting a course for being remarkable. Of course, the secret that no one will tell you is that being remarkable is the by-product, the result of doing everything you can to be the very best you can be. There is no specific formula for being remarkable; instead there are a series of seemingly insignificant things that, if done consistently, over time, will compound your results until those around you—customers, family, and community—take notice and are inclined to make a remark. Now that's remarkable!

CHAPTER 7   POWER POINTS

In this chapter we took a look at another obstacle to developing a strong framework for remarkable and to delivering and repeating remarkable performances. Here are some key points:

- Learn how to set a higher standard for yourself.
- Learn to keep promises to yourself.
- Learn to hold your own feet to the fire.
- Learn to see yourself as you really are.

Leader's Conversation Starter

Ask the members of your team to look at Figure 7.2 and assess the team for remarkable in the eyes of the team members and in the eyes of the customer. Then in the following two boxes, have them decide what actions they could take as individuals and as a team to increase their chances for delivering and repeating remarkable performances.

How remarkable are we today?	→	Very ... Sort of ... Not Very
How remarkable does our customer think we are today?	→	Very ... Sort of ... Not Very
What would make us more remarkable in our customer's eyes? If we did what?	→	1. 2. 3.
What would we need to start doing as a team to increase our customer's view of us?	→	1. 2. 3.

FIGURE 7.2 ■ Evaluating Remarkable

CHAPTER 8

The Most Difficult
Person to Lead

*The man who complains about the way the ball
bounces is likely the one who dropped it.*

—LOU HOLTZ

M Y SON took a job at Chick-fil-A. If you are not familiar with Chick-fil-A, it is a national chain of quick-serve restaurants specializing in everything chicken. The food is outstanding, but the service is remarkable; it makes you sit up and take notice. This is surprising since, like other fast-food restaurants, it is a business that depends heavily on young adults (teenagers) to make things run. And if you are in the habit of visiting other fast-food types of restaurants, you know that most of the time the only thing that is memorable is what went wrong—wrong with the food, wrong with the service, wrong with the environment. Well, the Chick-fil-A experience is exactly that, an experience. The company calls it that and takes pride in it. If you are there for only a few minutes, you sense the remarkable service, you see it, and you experience it. How can Chick-fil-A do this when the restaurants on either side of it, which get their talent from the same local talent pool of teenagers, can't even come close to what is going on at Chick-fil-A? The Chick-fil-A framework for remarkable performance is really something special, and it guides the company's business success.

I wanted to learn Chick-fil-A's secret, so one day I pulled aside the owner-operator, Margaret, and asked her how she was able to consistently hire such high-quality talent when the restaurants on either side of her store could not even come close. Margaret told me that some years earlier she witnessed a young man who worked for her going out of his way to make something right. She told me, "He just would not leave the task half done; he wanted to make it right." Then, kind of as an off-the-cuff remark, she said to him, "I'll bet you made your bed today." When the young man responded that he had, she asked if he made his bed every day. When he told her he did, she knew she was on to something.

A Navy SEAL Told Me To

This exchange with Margaret brought to mind a talk I had once heard where an ex-Navy SEAL, T. C. Cummings, had become a leadership coach and was coaching a young executive. When the young executive came to the meeting, he began complaining about all that was wrong in his life and blaming others for the issues he was facing. Mr. Cummings asked him if he had made his bed that morning. The executive being coached responded rather disgustedly, saying, "What's that got to do with anything?" "Did you make your bed?" Mr. Cummings asked him again. Finally, the young executive answered, "No." "Well," said Mr. Cummings, "I want you to make your bed, starting tomorrow, for seven straight days and then come and see me next week." There was a little more pushback from the young man, but he finally agreed to do it. One week later when the executive returned, he was a changed man. As Mr. Cummings tells the story, the young man said that he now understood and that he got the point. And what was the point? The point, according to Mr. Cummings, was to start your day with an action and to take personal responsibility for your surroundings. In essence, lead yourself exceptionally well if you ever expect to be able to lead others.

Now, let's go back to Margaret at Chick-fil-A. Margaret then asked me if I had made my bed. "I did make my bed today," I told her. I make it every day, even when I am traveling and in a hotel room. At home, my wife will beat me to it sometimes, but it never goes unmade. On the road, I have probably shocked more than one hotel maid as he or she came into the room to find the bed made and the room in order. This is not a habit I have always had—just ask my mom—but it is one that I developed when I decided to take my life to the next level. I needed order and I needed focus. As Margaret tells it, "Bed-makers are doers, not dreamers. They seem happier and more focused. They are finishers who are highly organized. They think ahead."

The Most Difficult Person to Lead Is Me

When I combined what Margaret was telling me from her experience in the restaurant and what I learned from T. C. Cummings, I saw a clear connection between being remarkable and making your bed. Well, I should say I saw a connection in how personal leadership skills and the characteristics of bed makers are related to someone who consistently delivers remarkable performances. I believe that someone who takes the 45 seconds or so that it takes to make his or her bed each day is *demonstrating a mindset and a discipline that leads to greater things in life.*

Now, you may be asking yourself, "Is he saying that people who don't make their bed every day will not be as successful?" Of course not, but I do believe that the people who consistently deliver remarkable performances and enjoy amazing success are the people who also exhibit strong personal leadership.

At IBM, as well as most other successful companies, it is important to have leaders (those with a title and those without a title) who can lead themselves incredibly well. At IBM, we expect our leaders to own their area of the business and make decisions as if they were the CEO. This means taking responsibility for every process and every detail. To become the remarkable leader you need to become in order to lead remarkable performance, you do not have the luxury of deciding *not* to do some things because they are beneath you or are seemingly unimportant. Leaders with strong personal leadership qualities go out of their way to do the things that lead to success, and in doing so they provide an example to others to do the same.

The Remarkable Qualities of a Bed Maker

In this section of the book where we are talking about the framework part of our Model for Remarkable, I can't emphasize enough the importance of leading yourself well. The character qualities of a bed maker are the same strong personal leadership characteristics that differentiate remarkable performers from average performers. These qualities are life skills that put you on and keep you on the pathway to remarkable. Without them the ability to consistently deliver remarkable performances is significantly reduced.

Discipline Is Essential

The first characteristic that bed makers exhibit is *discipline*. This, as you will recall, is one of the four building blocks of our foundation and a key component of every remarkable performance. It has been said that successful people do the things unsuccessful people don't want to do. This reflects a discipline of doing the things that some people

KILLING MY INFLUENCE WITH OTHERS

Leading yourself well is one of the best ways I know to increase your positive influence with others. People want to follow people who inspire them, and leading yourself well is inspiring. But many times leaders can undo the positive influence with what I call *influence killers*. If you recognize any of these in your own life, take action immediately to change course and restore your positive influence with others.

a. Poor responses to changing circumstances
b. Emotional outbursts
c. Inappropriate language
d. Disrespectful comments about others
e. Never listen

think are too hard or too time consuming to do. People who make their beds don't mind doing the things that unsuccessful people won't do. They are disciplined about performing the tough or uncomfortable things of life whether they feel like it or not. They are able to take a long-range view and delay their gratification in order to increase their chance of future success.

Diligence Is in the Details

Another important characteristic of a bed maker that you find in remarkable performers is *diligence*. A person who is diligent is attentive to details and persistent in doing the things that need to be done. People who make their bed every day don't necessarily like making the bed. I know I don't. But it needs to be done, and I might as well be the one to do it. A definition of diligence that I like is "persistent, personal attention." I love that! Let me break that down for you so you can grab hold of the power of this leadership trait.

Diligence is persistent, personal attention. *Persistent* speaks to a continuous effort, never letting up. There is no need for persistence if things happen quickly, smoothly, and easily the first time. When the going gets rough, persistence keeps plugging away. Persistence is not just a short-term quality but is best displayed over the long haul.

Diligence is persistent, personal attention. *Personal* says that only I can do it, not someone else in my place. This is not delegation. And certainly there is no shirking responsibility. I am taking this issue, this character quality, this vision, this goal, personally.

Diligence is persistent, personal attention. *Attention* is obvious; I am not ignoring something or allowing it to slide by. Many times when things are frustrating, or confusing, or difficult, our temptation is to escape. Turn on the TV. Surf the Internet. Think about nothing for a while. Distract yourself. Maybe it will go away or resolve itself somehow. That is far from diligence. Diligence is persistent, personal attention.[1]

Being Intentional Means Being Aware

The next quality I find in bed makers that is also found in remarkable performers is that they are *intentional*. A bed does not get made by accident, and neither do most of the activities that lead to being remarkable. Just like making my bed each day, accomplishing the right things that promote my success is part of my plan and something I *intentionally* do to succeed. To me, this is what being purpose driven is about. I cannot just casually float through my day. My ordered and intentional approach helps me to find and achieve my purpose. And as T. C. Cummings said, "It starts your day with an action," and that can never be a bad thing!

> *The willingness to accept responsibility for one's own life is the source from which self-respect springs.*
> —JOAN DIDION

Organization Is Key to Clear Thinking

Bed makers and remarkable performers are also *organized*. Having an unmade bed adds to the clutter and confusion of my home. By making the *choice* to make my bed each day, even in my hotel room, I establish an ordered living space that promotes clear and unencumbered thinking. This carries over to my workplace and the process of establishing the few critical tasks I need to accomplish each day to ensure my success. There have been studies that confirm that being organized and focused leads to more optimism and greater engagement in the workplace.

Serving Others Breeds Remarkable

You really can't be remarkable or be a consistent bed maker if you are not *servant-hearted*. A service orientation is an important building block in establishing personal leadership and influence in the lives of others. A person who makes the bed each day is a person who does not dismiss this as a menial task that someone else can do. It is an opportunity to serve and show others (those closest to you, by the way) that you hold them in high regard. If you won't do that for those in your own home, there is very little chance you are going to show that kind of honor and respect for those outside your home. Plus where else can you make this big an impact on those you love with an investment of the 45 seconds it actually takes to make a bed. I timed it, trust me!

Taking Action Is a Hallmark of Remarkable

Of course, being *action oriented* is an obvious quality of bed makers and remarkable performers. You can never achieve remarkable if you are not willing to choose a path and take action. Bed makers and remarkable performers see what needs to be done, and then they do it. They do not stand around waiting to be told what to do. This is actually one of the biggest obstacles for those who consistently come up short of remarkable. It is not that they don't know what needs to be done; they just don't do it. In the early years of my marriage, I would try to help after dinner by clearing the table and cleaning the dishes. This was obviously an action that needed to be taken, and I took it. I would rinse the dishes and stack them neatly on the counter just above the dishwasher and walk away. My wife politely informed me one evening that if I would simply open the dishwasher door and drop the dishes inside, this act of loving service to the family would truly be remarkable. However, leaving the job half done was not only unremarkable; it caused someone else to have to come and complete the task. Did I not see that the dishes needed to be put in the dishwasher? Of course not. It's just that if I opened the door and the dishes inside were clean, then they would need to be put away, and I really didn't sign up for all of that; I just wanted credit for getting the dishes to the door. This is not remarkable-worthy personal leadership. I learned that it takes about 20 seconds to put the dishes in the dishwasher, and if the dishwasher is full of clean dishes, it takes about 3 minutes to empty it and complete the task. You may think this is a silly example, but it is exactly what nonremarkable performers do every day on a much larger scale. I'll go this far, but I won't take the obvious next-step actions because it seems like too much trouble. Bed makers and remarkable performers are action takers that know what needs to be done and then do it.

The Bed Makers at IBM

You may be asking yourself exactly how the qualities of personal leadership play out in the work environment. I know for a fact that at IBM we don't ask about your bed-making habits on the job application, but having strong personal leadership qualities is expected of every leader, whether you have the title of leader or not—in fact, much of the remarkable work is done by people without the title of leader. If an individual is not disciplined, diligent, intentional, or organized, is not willing to serve, and is not an action taker, then he or she will not succeed in leading at IBM, or anywhere for that matter.

In a global enterprise of over 400,000 employees, IBM expects its leaders to work across business units or divisional lines to solve problems. Leaders are expected to treat every person with respect, honor diversity in the workforce, and increase the ability to succeed and achieve remarkable results. But this cannot happen unless leaders can lead themselves well and in doing so increase their ability to influence others in a positive way. It is this ability to influence others that is at the core of leadership—so much of a leader's success at IBM or any large organization is dependent on the ability to influence others. The reason: if you cannot positively influence others, then you cannot get things done. To sum it up, leading yourself well increases your ability to influence others, and your ability to positively influence others is what will move you in the direction of achieving remarkable results.

One of the three IBM basic beliefs is "trust and personal responsibility in every relationship." I think that pretty much captures the importance of how you lead you. Take personal responsibility for how you lead yourself, and trust will increase in every relationship you have—your relationship with your team, your peers, and your customers. Increase trust, and you increase your potential for remarkable results.

CHAPTER 8 POWER POINTS

This chapter has been about you becoming a leader who knows the importance of leading yourself extremely well. You cannot consistently lead a team into remarkable performances if you are not willing to lead yourself into remarkable performances. The key message from this chapter is:

- Personal leadership, as exhibited in people who make their beds, is the differentiator between remarkable leaders and average leaders.

Leader's Conversation Starter

Have each of the members of your team answer the following questions. Once they have completed their personal assessment, facilitate a group discussion having the individual members share from their list of ideas.

1. What traits and characteristics show you that people lead themselves extremely well?
   a. _____
   b. _____
   c. _____
   d. _____

2. How can you tell that people do *not* lead themselves well?
   a. _____
   b. _____

3. What one thing could you do in your life to exhibit greater personal leadership? (This might be an area where you know you cut corners or you know you should but don't.)

_____

CHAPTER 9

Fighting the Resistance

Most of us have two lives. The life we live and the unlived life within us. Between the two stands Resistance.

—STEVEN PRESSFIELD

Resistance to What?

WHEN YOU are developing a strong framework where you will construct all your remarkable performances, it is important to recognize and call out this thing known as the *resistance*. Author Seth Godin wrote, "The resistance is working overtime to be sure that you won't actually do anything remarkable. As a result, the list of excuses in reverse is longer than you might expect." There is a great truth here for anyone wanting to deliver or lead others to deliver remarkable performances—there will always be a list of excuses designed to keep you from repeating success. You will face this resistance, and you won't really know that's what it is unless you train yourself to recognize what it looks like.

So what is this "resistance"? Resistance is the enemy inside you that keeps you from performing your art. Art? You say, "I'm not an artist." We are all artists in one form or another. Your art may be teaching a class or running a business; you could be selling, or you could be leading. Artists are people who can make the world a better place by using their gifts and talents to deliver a remarkable performance. The resistance inside you is empowered by a fear or anxiety that you may not have what it takes or that what you are able to deliver is not good enough. The resistance is everywhere you turn. When you start a new diet, you find excuses for not following it. When you commit to a delivery date for a project, you find other things to occupy your time. When you need to sit down and plan, create, or innovate each day, why are there suddenly dozens of reasons to delay the start of actually doing it? That's the resistance; and it hinders your art, and it destroys your potential for remarkable.

Defeating the Resistance

Honestly, it's highly unlikely you can completely defeat the resistance, but you can battle it head-on and win—today. The single most important step you can engage in to take back the ground the resistance has taken from you is to recognize that there is a resistance. Call it by name. Say it out loud. I will do this when I sit down to work on a project and I feel the urge to check the sports scores from last night. "That's the resistance!" I say out loud. I get out my files, and I am tempted to go refresh my coffee and see what my boss is doing. "That's the resistance!" After sharing these ideas with a friend of mine, I saw him send a twitter message stating, "Well played resistance, well played, but I am not falling for it this time!" Recognizing that it is there and that it is real is the only way to begin a successful defense of your art.

Your art is what you do when no one can tell you exactly how to do it. Your art is the act of taking personal responsibility, challenging the status quo, and changing people.
—SETH GODIN

The second step to defeat the resistance is to just start. Once you recognize that the resistance is in you and is strong, the only way you can move past it is to just start doing your work. If it is writing, then start writing. If it is preparation for a speech, then begin the preparation. It sounds silly, but the role of the resistance is to keep you from starting, so start.

Turning Pro

Another thing you can do to defeat the resistance is to begin to look at yourself as a "professional." Author Steven Pressfield, in his excellent book on the resistance called *The War of Art*,[1] says, "The professional tackles the project that will make him stretch. He takes on the assignment that will bear him into uncharted waters, compel him to explore unconscious parts of himself." He goes on to describe the difference between an amateur and a professional, "The amateur plays for fun. The professional plays for keeps. The amateur plays part-time, the professional full-time. The amateur is a weekend warrior. The professional is there seven days a week."[2] Are you a professional? At first I had trouble considering myself a professional, but as I considered Pressfield's point, it occurred to me that the only way I could deliver the results I was hoping to deliver—remarkable results—was to change my mindset to that of a professional and stop thinking like an amateur.

The resistance is generally the strongest after you have enjoyed some success. It's almost like you give yourself permission to be distracted because you know you have successfully navigated these waters before. The great lesson here for each of us is to acknowledge that there is a resistance inside of us and that we need to face it directly if we hope to have a chance of delivering and repeating remarkable performances.

Winning Your Future

As a global leader, IBM has many talented leaders around the world. One of the great messages I heard delivered by a key European leader to his team had to do with calling the members of his team to a higher standard that he felt was necessary for them to accomplish what they were capable of accomplishing as an IBM division. He said, we must "win the future." He continued by saying that "to get there, we can't just stand still." He concluded by reminding the team members that nothing would be given to them. Their goals could only be accomplished by hard work and determination. This is actually a great lesson from

IBM's history. Over the 100-year history of the company, there are many examples of "winning the future." I think the most memorable was the transition from a hardware company of the 1990s to the software and services company of the new millennium. The leaders at the time decided that for IBM to compete and win in the future, it would need to be more responsive to customer needs and actually provide solutions that solved customer problems. That may sound incredibly obvious, but it was a clear decision point in the mid-1990s that turned IBM away from impending disaster and set it on a remarkable course of recovery.

How true this is for all of us desiring to build a strong framework for remarkable and stay the course after a success or string of successes. As we continue to develop our framework for our model of remarkable performances and as we achieve our goals and enjoy our success, we need to remember that no one gave the success to us as a gift; we worked hard for it. This becomes even truer when you begin the next journey and desire to repeat your success. Not only will it not be handed to you, but as we have been discussing, there will be additional obstacles.

When I consider the IBM leader's words about winning the future, I want to apply that to you and what it takes to ensure that you win your future—and that you help your team members win their future. What kind of actions would be required for this to happen? This brings up another question: Is this some sort of competition? If I win my future, does someone have to lose a future? Obviously the answer is no; the future is not a zero-sum game. But it is a bit of a competition. The person you are competing with is you! It is so tempting sometimes to just stand still and let the future come to you, but that is not how futures are won, not for remarkable performers.

It's Easy Not to Do

Jim Rohn once said, "The things we need to do to be successful are easy to do, they are also easy not to do." As it turns out, your greatest competition to being and delivering remarkable is you. It will be you that keeps you from winning your future. Unless you are willing to intentionally and proactively do the things that need to be done, when they need to be done, you will join the armies of average performers. You will not stay the course.

If you are serious about delivering remarkable performances, you need to decide today that you will take control of your future. Keeping to the course that got you to this point will more than likely not be enough to take you where you want to be in the future, especially if remarkable is your goal. Winning the future means to set, strive for, and reach the goals and dreams you have for yourself. If that is to happen, then you will need to take some specific steps to ensure that it does. This is a key component of the training that IBM leaders receive. Winning the future for these leaders means achieving the targets that have been set before them each quarter and each year. To ensure these leaders have a clear plan for achieving all their goals, we ask them to consider a small set of steps necessary for winning. When they do these few seemingly insignificant things, then we know that they are on their way to success.

The first step for winning your future is to *decide what winning looks like.* This is part of the foundation for our Model for Remarkable. What is your goal or vision of where you want to be and what you want to be doing 5, 10, 15, or more years down the road? IBM managers are each given a clear set of metrics to use to measure progress, but deciding what winning looks like is often about more than just metrics. We also ask our leaders to consider what winning looks like for the development of individuals on their team, what winning looks like for the climate they provide for their team, and what winning looks like for themselves personally and their development as a leader. By having this locked down, you will be able to chart your course. Otherwise you are likely to be driven and tossed by the circumstances that come your way. Drifting is a guaranteed way to *not* win your future. You are where you are today because of the decisions and actions you made five years ago. Where you are five years from now will depend on the decisions and actions you take today.

Another important component of winning your future is to *remind yourself early and often that you have what it takes* to be remarkable and deliver remarkable performances. Develop a discipline of no negative self-talk; by self-talk, I mean you talking to you. You may not be aware of this, but from the moment we rise each day until we hit the bed each night, we have a running conversation going on inside our heads. Every thought and idea that you have is a form of how you talk to yourself and how you feel about you and the things you are doing or are capable of doing. You can tell yourself positive things all day long, or you can tell yourself negative things all day long. These might be things like how you feel about your abilities to handle a task or attempt something new. It might be things like how you feel about your age and physical appearance. Either way, this is where your belief in you comes from and has a lot to do with the level of self-confidence you have in yourself. It also has a lot to do with what you communicate subconsciously to others. IBM leaders are in general very self-assured. They often put on an overly self-confident outer shell, but as with many in the leadership community, the outer shell and the inner self don't always match up. I always ask leaders to monitor how they are speaking to themselves and to be intentional about reminding themselves that they have what it takes to do this. Positive self-talk is often overlooked as an important component of delivering remarkable performances. How you talk to yourself matters greatly in positioning yourself to succeed. The way that negative self-talk is often revealed in leaders is in how they talk about their performance shortfalls. If there are phrases like "I didn't think...," "I never thought...," I couldn't...," or "It wasn't possible to...," then you might have a self-talk problem. Refer to the sidebar and the C.R.E.D.I.T. model for some ideas on how to address this important issue.

If you really want to ensure that you win your future, then you need to embrace the truth that *you can control how you invest today.* I work with a lot of individuals who do not fully accept that they can control what happens in the future by paying close attention to how they manage today. Today is the future of 5 years ago. I am where I am today and I am who I am today because of the actions, activities, and people I was with 5 years ago. Did I know that then? Where I am going to be 5 or 10 years from now will be a direct result of the

GIVE YOURSELF A LITTLE C.R.E.D.I.T.

How you talk to yourself matters. If you are not fully aware of this conversation with yourself going on in your head, then spend a day or two tracking what the internal conversation is about. Often it is negative and discouraging. To change that conversation to one that is positive and encouraging, give yourself a little C.R.E.D.I.T.

C.—challenge yourself. Most negative talk stems from feelings of inferiority when facing new challenges. It could be from a fear of failing or of embarrassing yourself. Remind yourself that this is part of growing and becoming better. Embrace the challenge.

R.—remind yourself. A lot of negative self-talk comes from remembering past failures. Remind yourself that the past is gone forever and the lessons you learned are helping you to be better today.

E.—encourage yourself. When I see others struggling with something, I am always the first to encourage them that they can do it. Why don't I do that for me? When you notice a negative thought, capture it and then give yourself an encouraging word. You have what it takes!

D.—discipline yourself. Negative talk can also come from a feeling of failure for not doing the things you know you should do to succeed. You didn't read that article; you didn't get up an hour earlier to prepare, etc. Do the things you are supposed to do when you are supposed to do them. Developing this discipline will remove a lot of negative talk.

I.—improve yourself. Some of the negative self-talk comes from feelings of inadequacy. You need to realize that you have not arrived; you are always growing, learning, and improving. Develop a plan for growth and improvement, and let your self-talk be encouraging that you are taking those steps.

T.—transform yourself. To be transformed is to be changed. Take pride and be encouraged that you are taking the steps to be a better version of your past self. No matter what your starting point may have been, we all need to be constantly transforming ourselves through constant, steady improvement.

actions, activities, and people I am around today. How you choose to spend your today will determine how you will spend your tomorrows. This is a challenge for leaders at IBM and elsewhere. The demands on your calendar today and the choices you make about those demands will determine the outcomes you enjoy. As part of our leader training at IBM, we always encourage leaders to make wise choices about how they invest today. The results they generate are directly related to the choices they have made with their time.

> *It was character that got us out of bed, commitment that moved us into action, and discipline that enabled us to follow through.*
> —ZIG ZIGLAR

The key for managing your "today" is to have a plan for where you want to go and how you intend to get there. Author and speaker Dr. John C. Maxwell talks often of not waiting until you are in the battle to make the decisions. Instead, *decide early* what you will do and then *manage those decisions daily*. If you are trying to lose weight, you need to make a couple of critical decisions about what you are going to eat and when and how you are going to exercise. Then all you have to do is execute those decisions every day. However, if you do not make those two critical decisions early, but wait instead to make them every day, you will have a reduced chance of actually doing what you set out to do. You will be swayed by the circumstances and how you feel about the circumstance, which normally leads to a bag of Oreos.

We often remind our IBM leaders that there is no silver bullet or fast path to winning your future. If you hope to stay the course and continually deliver remarkable performances, you are going to have to make a plan to do that and then work your plan daily. This is why we train to the weekly one-on-one and team cadence reviews. The few critical success factors have already been determined, and now these leaders must help their teams to execute on each element on a daily basis. The one-on-one review (mentioned in Chapter 2) is probably the single best way I have seen for leaders to maintain clarity and focus with their team. A simple 30-minute call each week is all it takes to ensure everyone is moving in the same direction. The weekly cadence review is something IBM uses to make sure the sales team is taking all appropriate actions needed to move customer opportunities forward. It is done in a team format to allow everyone the opportunity to contribute to the progress and success of the team. The process is simple and allows everyone to focus on the select few critical actions needed to move each opportunity forward. The reason so many people miss remarkable is not for lack of desire to deliver remarkable, but for lack of consistency in executing a plan that leads to remarkable.

Winning the future at IBM has not always been a guaranteed thing. There were times in the mid-1990s when the future was completely up for grabs. With billion-dollar losses and a failing business model, it was not clear if IBM would even be in the future, much less win the future. What changed was the decision by our leadership team to intentionally put the disciplines in place to ensure we were positioned as a company to win. From the top of the organization down, this meant developing and communicating a new strategy around software and services. From the bottom of the organization up, this meant having the employees individually agree with their local leadership team on what was their personal commitment to helping their business unit within IBM achieve its goals. It was then the daily managing of thousands of personal business commitments that allowed IBM the opportunity to achieve the remarkable results it is once again enjoying.

CHAPTER 9 POWER POINTS

In order to make remarkable a regular part of who you are, it is important to recognize and rebuke the force inside of you known as the resistance. On the surface it seems that once you have been successful at something, it should be easy to repeat that success, but my experience, and the experience of those I coach, is not that at all. The resistance loves to raise its head when you are attempting to do your best work, and it loves to derail someone who has previously enjoyed some success. Some things to remember include:

- **Fighting the resistance.** The natural tendency to be distracted by other things can easily derail you when you are trying to stay on track.
- **Winning your future.** The only real way to stay the course, even if you have been enjoying success, is to set a vision for your future and take the necessary steps to get there.

Leader's Conversation Starter

Ask the members of your team to answer the following questions on their own and then have the members each share their answers with the group. This is a great way to uncover some of the thoughts and feelings that often undermine your best intentions to stay the course. If you do not have a team, you may answer these questions for yourself.

1. Have you ever noticed this thing we call "the resistance" when you are trying to perform your art? If so, what form did it take?___

   _____

   _____

2. List three ways or actions you can take to overcome the resistance when you find that it is trying to derail your work._____

   _____

   _____

This Is Your Masterpiece

It is the capacity to develop and improve their skills
that distinguishes leaders from followers.

—WARREN BENNIS

F YOU have ever had the opportunity to read any of the writings of legendary UCLA basketball coach John Wooden, then you have most likely read how he challenged his players to make each day a masterpiece. Coach Wooden would remind his players that you cannot give 80 percent effort today because you had a bad night last night or your girlfriend broke up with you and then give 120 percent tomorrow to make up for it. All you can give in any 24-hour period is 100 percent. Anything you leave on the table is lost forever; you cannot reclaim it tomorrow. With that truth in mind, he then told his team to "make each day your masterpiece."

As we look further at the framework for remarkable performances, this idea that you are creating a masterpiece connects with all four of our framework building blocks of being exceptional, being disciplined, being prepared, and being persistent. In order to develop an intentional approach that would help you work toward delivering remarkable performances, I would like to present a disciplined daily approach that will increase your ability to make each day a masterpiece. My goal is to help you to develop a mindset that will allow you to accomplish remarkable results no matter what the challenge might be. To do that, I developed a simple yet effective approach to making everyday a masterpiece.

Don't measure yourself by what you have accomplished, but by what you should have accomplished with your ability.
—JOHN WOODEN

The Starting Point for Today Is Yesterday

When working with IBM leaders about making every day a masterpiece, it becomes very obvious very early that we are dealing with a distraction-filled environment. I am guessing this is a challenge in most corporate environments. There is no shortage of things to do and no shortage of things to interrupt your day. The key to building a masterpiece is to be disciplined about your approach and intentional in your execution.

The starting point for making every day your masterpiece is to *start your day the night before.* The single most important step you can take to position yourself for remarkable performances is to never go to bed without laying out your plan for the following day. The real power here is in determining what your "big rocks" are for the next day and deciding when you are going to work on them. The way I do this is to make a plan the night before that defines specifically what will be the first three things that I will do the next morning.

Having this all decided in advance does several things. One, it will help you sleep better. There is no need for your mind to work on what you are going to do in the morning when you get up; it is already decided. Two, it helps you overcome the desire to stay in bed the next morning. If you have a plan to rise at 5 A.M. (as you will see below, I advocate rising early), read for 30 minutes, write for 1 hour, and then go for a run before showering and getting to work, you will not lie in bed under warm covers trying to make a plan with your eyes closed. Every night, before getting in the bed, you look at your calendar for the following day; you set out your workout clothes; and you have your books, e-reader, or whatever you plan to read or write with laid out where you will sit down the next morning to start your day. This is a

SKIP SLEEP, HAVE A STROKE!

As noted in *USA Today*, "The 30 percent of working adults who routinely sleep less than six hours a night are four times more likely to suffer a stroke."[1]

Researchers at the University of Alabama concluded that:

- Only 28 percent of adults get more than eight hours of sleep per night
- As many as 30 percent of adults get less than six hours of sleep per night
- You are four times more likely to have a stroke when getting less than six hours per night

seemingly insignificant step, but if performed consistently over time, it will compound the potential of your day to be a masterpiece and your performance to be remarkable. If you leave the start of the day to chance and feeling, staying in bed becomes one of your options, and it will be the winning option more times than any of us cares to admit.

An often overlooked component of increasing your potential for remarkable performances also takes place the night before, and that component is to *get your rest*. For years I was in the habit of getting as little sleep as possible. I developed a pride around the fact that I could function quite well on four hours of sleep a night. Then I began to do some reading and studying of diet and exercise books, and I discovered that getting your rest was an integral part of a balanced approach to managing your health. You can actually improve weight loss and fitness while you are asleep. New research, recently released, has found that getting less than six hours of sleep a night can increase your chances of having a stroke (see the sidebar "Skip Sleep, Have a Stroke!"). Many people stay up until one or two in the morning playing video games or watching TV. Then they have to be at work at 8 A.M., and they wonder why they just can't get more done and why they get so far behind. My solution to this dilemma is to return to what my parents taught me when I was eight years old—have a preset bedtime.

Your 24-Hour Day

A simple exercise that I often ask IBM leaders to complete is something you can use to arrange your day with the express goal of making every day a masterpiece. I call the exercise "My 24-Hour Day" (see Figure 10.1 for an example), and it is very useful for determining how you will intentionally use the 24 hours you have been given. The response from most of the leaders who complete this exercise is disbelief about where they actually spend their time. The exercise goes like this:

a. Take a blank sheet of paper.
b. At the top of the paper, write "12 A.M."
c. At the bottom of the paper, write "12 A.M."
d. In the middle of the paper, write "Noon."
e. You now have a 24-hour calendar; if you want to list specific hours, you may certainly do so now.
f. Begin to draw boxes on the 24-hour calendar that represent how you will generally spend your time. See Figure 10.1 so you know what I mean.

For example:

- In Figure 10.1, I drew a box that spans 8 A.M. to 6 P.M., indicating the general hours that I would devote to my job. This may move on the calendar, but in general terms that is the time I will allocate for my work.
- Next, I drew a box that goes from 6 P.M. to 10 P.M., and I called this "Home/Family/Life." This is when I will be home for dinner with the family, devote time to being with the family, and do any other types of activities that fall outside of work. This has a lot of flexibility depending on all the different directions my family may go on any given evening. Whatever we do, I want to allocate the time to my family—and if I get some of that back for me, then I can deal with that when it happens.
- Next I decided when I would like to get out of bed each day— 5 A.M.—and so I drew a box between 5 A.M. and 8 A.M. Your

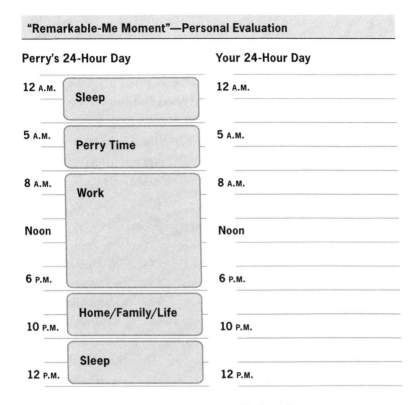

"Remarkable-Me Moment"—Personal Evaluation

Perry's 24-Hour Day

12 A.M.
Sleep
5 A.M.
Perry Time
8 A.M.
Work
Noon
6 P.M.
Home/Family/Life
10 P.M.
Sleep
12 P.M.

Your 24-Hour Day

12 A.M.
5 A.M.
8 A.M.
Noon
6 P.M.
10 P.M.
12 P.M.

FIGURE 10.1 ■ Your 24-Hour Day

time to rise may be different, but I believe wholeheartedly, as you will read in the next section, that getting up at a set time every day is important.

- That leaves 10 P.M. to 5 A.M. for sleep—a nice 7-hour block of time dedicated to getting my rest.

What you will learn from this simple exercise is that you have a lot more time available than you previously thought you did. In my case I learned that I can actually do anything I want to do between 10 P.M. and 8 A.M. That's 10 hours. Wow! The key to using this incredible chunk of time for making remarkable masterpieces is to use it intentionally. Prior to waking up to this truth (pun intended), I was just defaulting through this time slot every day. Not sleeping enough, not reading enough, not exercising at all, just kind of mindlessly floating through and exclaiming far too often, "I don't have time" or "I don't know where my time goes."

To make every day your masterpiece and position yourself to deliver remarkable performances, you need to get out of the bed each day with authority and purpose. To do this it is best to have a preset bedtime and a preset rise time and then to be disciplined enough to obey those presets. You cannot make a masterpiece if you are limiting your sleep. Get your rest and be ready to go when the bell rings.

We're All Morning People

I have already mentioned that I *rise early* because it is perhaps one of the more meaningful things I do that gives me a strategic advantage when it comes to delivering a remarkable performance. If you spend time with people you consider to be remarkable, I guarantee that somewhere in their list of things that helped them get there is having a set time to get out of bed every day. The way I chose the time I wanted to get out of bed was based on the 24-hour-day calendar calculation in the exercise we just completed. Based on when I need to be at work and when I am going to get my 7 hours of sleep, I chose 5 A.M. This 3-hour window provides me an extra 21+ hours a week that most of my colleagues don't get to experience. This also allows me to never have to say, "I don't have time." One critical success factor in taking this action step is to determine early how you are going to invest this time. Remember, we are developing our canvas for making today our masterpiece with the express desire of being able to deliver and repeat remarkable performances. How you manage today is a critical component to how your framework contributes to your being remarkable. So how will you invest your time? Here is how I do it, but you should have your own list of priorities. Take a moment to fill in some ideas in Figure 10.2.

When completing this exercise with IBM leaders, we often make an agreement that you can no longer use the words *I didn't have the time.* The only acceptable phrasing from this point forward is *I didn't take the time.* Once a leader has made this mental transition, it becomes a

"Remarkable-Me Moment"—Personal Evaluation	
My Five O'Clock Club Priorities	Your ___ O'Clock Club Priorities
1. Inspirational reading/study	1. _____
2. Reading/study personal development material	2. _____
	3. _____
3. Writing/idea capture	4. _____
4. Exercise	

FIGURE 10.2 ▪ The Five O'Clock Club

powerful leadership tool. It speaks strongly to how you lead yourself, and it is an amazing example to your team about the expectations you are setting forth for others.

Two-thirds of my time is spent on filling my mind with good things to help me grow in spiritual and professional ways. One-third of my time is spent on exercise to help me grow physically. Actually, before I started doing this, I was growing physically, but it was all focused around my waistline, and it was not good. I have also found an added bonus during the exercise time. I use my MP3 device to listen to audiobooks and podcasts while I work out. Sometimes these are biographies and leadership books, and sometimes they are fiction just for fun. This has really helped me stay committed to the exercise part of my morning, because I feel that I am getting double use from the time I am on the treadmill or stair climber.

After giving this talk to a group of business owners, a gentleman in a chef's outfit came to speak to me and tell me how I had inspired him and how he was going to totally commit himself to getting up at 5 A.M. so he could be more productive and begin reading and developing his skills. His wife, also in a chef's outfit, stood next to him shaking her head. When I asked why she was shaking her head, she explained that they ran a catering business, that much of their work ran late into the evening, and that they often did not get home until after midnight. It occurred to me immediately that he thought my message was that to be remarkable at what you do and to make every day a masterpiece, you have to get out of bed at 5 A.M. I immediately changed how I present this topic, and I explained to him that there is nothing magical about 5 A.M. It's magical for me but would be disastrous for him. So I asked him when his most productive time of the day was, and he told me that he was on fire between midnight and 3 A.M. Ouch! I thought (but did not say out loud). I asked him how he spent that time today, and he said he would watch some TV, listen to some music, or play with his video game console. We spent the remainder of our time talking about a more intentional use of his most productive hours, and he made a commitment to redesigning his 24-hour day.

Please hear me—I am not telling you to get up at 5 A.M. I am telling you that *I* get up at 5 A.M. and that it works magic in my life to have that additional time each week and to use it in ways that help me to grow and develop. Do the exercise in Figure 10.1 to determine your best time and then commit to making it meaningful and doing it every day.

I am often asked what I mean by "every day." Hmmm, I mean "every" day. Here is how the conversation usually goes:

THEM: What do you mean by "every day"?
ME: I mean I do this every day.
THEM: But what about the weekends?
ME: Every day!
THEM: But what about, like, holidays?
ME: Every day!
THEM: Christmas?
ME: *I stare at them and stay silent.*
THEM: Your birthday?
ME: EVERY DAY!

It is because of questioning sequences like this one that you begin to see part of the problem with being able to consistently deliver remarkable performances. It is in our human nature to gravitate to what is the least I can do to make this work. You will quickly learn that if you can determine the disciplined steps you need to take and then take them *every day*, you will be well on your way to delivering the kind of performance you desire to deliver. Consistency is vital to being remarkable.

Working the Plan

Another important discipline of remarkable performers is that they *work their plan for the day*. I mentioned earlier that the IBM leaders I work with are in a distraction-filled environment. When I began looking at how they work their plan for the day, I found a great deal of starting and stopping and very little focus on the most important tasks facing them that day. Dr. Stephen Covey has a beautiful example of how to work your plan for the day. He calls it "Big Rocks First."[2] If you are going to develop your ability to deliver and lead remarkable performances, you are going to need to develop the habit of performing your most important tasks (big rocks) in the most productive part of your day. For me this is first thing in the morning. There is often a temptation to rush into trivial, less important tasks like checking my e-mail or looking at social media sites, because they give the illusion that I am accomplishing something. This is the resistance we spoke about earlier. I might be checking things off a list, but they mean very little in the scope of what I am really trying to accomplish. Focus on the important tasks first. You cannot build a masterpiece, establish a strong framework, or deliver a remarkable performance if you don't build and execute a plan for your day—every day.

> *The key is not to prioritize what's on your schedule, but to schedule your priorities.*
> —DR. STEPHEN COVEY

Working your plan for the day is important, but only if you also take a few minutes to *prioritize* all the tasks you have in your plan. Reject the temptation to rush into low-priority tasks. It's tempting because they make us feel like we are getting a lot of things done. I like to pick the single most important task of the day and work on it until it is complete. Then go to the second most important task, and so on. To do this you must know which are the most important tasks and put them in sequence of how they should be accomplished. I use a method that I have heard called the *ABCDE* method.[3] You begin by taking everything you need to accomplish in a given day or week and give it a priority ranking.

A tasks would be the most important tasks, *B* tasks would be the next most important, and *C* tasks would be the third most important tasks to be accomplished. You would never do a *B*-rated task before all the *A*-rated tasks are completed. *D* stands for "delegate." These are tasks that should be handed to someone else more suited to accomplish the work. *E* stands for "eliminate." These are tasks you should not be doing at all. You may think there are none of these on your task list, but there are. I know this because most of us have trouble saying no to things we should say no to, and so we end up doing things we have

BE HERE NOW!

After returning home from a long road trip, I found that my wife had gone to my home office and removed a small placard I had on my desk and placed it on the kitchen counter. The placard read BE HERE NOW. When she saw me staring at the sign, she asked me if I believed that sign or was it just decoration for my desk. Busted!

What my wife wanted me to know was that when I came home, she wanted me home. She didn't want to see me stealing glances at my BlackBerry or other devices while I was in a conversation with her or our children. *Be here now.*

That sign was on my desk to remind me to focus on one task at a time, especially when people are involved. Don't multitask when you are on the phone. *Be here now.*

Be here now is not only a reminder to focus and not multitask; it is a reminder to honor others and show value to others by engaging them without distraction. What changes would you need to make in your life in order to place more focus on the tasks you are trying to accomplish?

no business doing. Developing this discipline will raise the level of the work you do and put you well on your way to developing a masterpiece each day.

As part of the training at IBM, we ask leaders to consider scheduling things like reading and responding to e-mail and returning phone calls. We try to have our leaders develop the discipline of checking e-mail twice a day and returning phone calls once a day. This is in sharp contrast to what many of us do, which is checking our e-mail continually and returning phone calls throughout the day. You have a reduced chance of generating a remarkable performance with that kind of constant distraction.

Who Me? Multitask?

Another temptation that we must all overcome is the temptation to multitask. *Don't multitask*. We live in a world that teaches multitasking at a ridiculously early age. Most of us are doctorate-level performers in multitasking. Unfortunately, research shows that if we jump from task to task, we end up doing multiple things poorly. At first, all the IBM leaders I share this with reject this research because they feel good about their work, and they actually feel that they are getting more done because they are doing multiple things at one time. The truth is that even though they are not producing bad work, they have a reduced chance of being remarkable. I often have to remind them that the goal is not to see how much you can get done, but to achieve remarkable results from your team and for your customer. They often admit that it sometimes feels like success if they get to the end of their e-mail. Nothing could be further from the truth.

An often overlooked step in building a masterpiece and delivering remarkable performances is to set aside some time to *rejuvenate*. To remain focused you need regular breaks to step away for a few minutes and rejuvenate your mind and body. Take a walk. Get away from your work area. This was (is) tough for me. But again, research shows that allowing yourself a few minutes to reenergize is a great way to keep focus and energy on the tasks you are trying to accomplish.

THE BREAK-90 RULE

I have established a simple rule around my office that I call the Break-90 Rule. I put this in place to remind myself not to sit in one place for hour after hour without taking a few minutes to rejuvenate myself. To provide an environment for this to happen, I break my work into 90-minute segments. I do my very best to work distraction free for 90 minutes and then take a 10- to 15-minute break. During my break I like to:

- Get a bottle of water
- Walk outside if at all possible
- Do some stretching

Once I have completed this simple ritual, I return to my desk ready to go for the next 90 minutes. Try it; you will notice a difference in the intensity of your work.

To differentiate yourself in any environment, you must always *be prepared and stay engaged.* By staying engaged, I mean staying involved, being present. An important part of the leadership training provided to IBMers is the lesson of always arriving prepared to the many meetings and conference calls they have each day. The overriding message is that you should come prepared with your point of view on the topic being discussed. Every IBMer, leader with a title or without, is encouraged to remain engaged in the conversation. I have seen this tested when the leader of a call or meeting will wait until whoever was presenting has finished speaking. Then the leader will ask another participant, "Bob, what do you think?" The leader knows that there are many distractions competing for our attention. He is trying to train us to fight distraction and remain engaged. It is unacceptable behavior to not have a point of view, and it is an enormous no-no to have to ask someone to repeat what was being talked about. Do your homework, be prepared, and be provocative. Come with a point of view and be ready to defend it. Remarkable performers are not the type to stay quiet and not interject ideas or solutions into the mix. Remarkable performers always have a point of view.

Look, Shiny Things!

To really be effective and get the most value from your investment of time, you must find a way to *minimize distractions.* I will talk more about combating distraction in a later chapter, but for now let me just say that this seems to be one of the largest wrecking balls that our framework for remarkable will face. Distractions often come in the form of the technologies you use to run your life. Remarkable performers learn to manage their workspace and manage their technology. Most people forget that their mobile devices have an on-off switch. Set up your workspace in a way that distractions are minimized. Situate where you sit in such a way as to reduce the distraction caused by other people and movements. Turn off e-mail beeps and phone buzzes. Put that instant messaging software on "do not disturb." If you don't proactively establish a distraction-free work zone, you will be constantly fighting the battle for your attention. Remarkable performances are the reward of focused people.

Of course, there will be setbacks, so you will need to *evaluate your day.* No one gets it right every day, so take every opportunity to evaluate your progress and make adjustments as necessary. Determine what worked and what didn't and make changes accordingly.

As part of our sales leader enablement at IBM, we try to instill a "daily masterpiece" mindset in each of our leaders. We know that doing the fundamentals correctly, day in and day out, is what leads to remarkable results. The ability to get our leaders into this mindset is the difference maker when it comes to achieving remarkable. If you don't do the daily disciplines that we have discussed in this chapter, then you open the door for average performance. If our leaders do not focus on the big rocks of our business and manage their time and resources effectively, then we will have a very small chance of achieving the remarkable results that IBM asks us to achieve every year.

SAMETIME

At IBM we have a productivity tool called Sametime that every IBMer is strongly encouraged to use. Sametime is an instant messaging and collaboration tool that allows you to "ping" your coworkers worldwide and engage in a conversation in real time. It is truly amazing to think that I can click on your name and open a dialogue box when you are in Austria and I am in Atlanta and engage you in a conversation.

But as with most productivity tools, you need to manage the tool so the tool does not manage you. One way we teach our teams at IBM to manage the tools is to take advantage of the Do Not Disturb setting when they are focused on an important project. Many of our leaders actually encourage their people to use this feature when they are on a conference call so the participants may focus on the subject of the call without being interrupted.

I can't imagine running our business without the use of the Sametime direct messaging and collaboration tool, but I also cannot imagine achieving remarkable results without managing the use of the tool to meet my specific needs.

CHAPTER 10 POWER POINTS

In this chapter we have looked more closely at the importance of taking seemingly insignificant yet intentional steps to make everything you do a masterpiece. Here are essential steps if you hope to have a strong framework and consistently deliver and repeat remarkable performances:

- Start the night before
- Get your rest—sleep matters
- Document your 24-hour day
- Rise earlier, or at least earlier

- Work your plan and prioritize
- Don't multitask
- Take time to rejuvenate and evaluate
- Be prepared and engaged
- Minimize distractions

Leader's Conversation Starter #1

After sharing the model in Figure 10.3, have your team do a stop doing–start doing–keep doing exercise around the components for making masterpieces. This is a great way to engage the members of your team in a conversation on the importance of taking the necessary personal actions to drive remarkable performances. Once they have completed their evaluation, have individual team members share some of their ideas with the rest of the team.

Masterpiece Components	Stop Doing	Start Doing	Keep Doing
Before I go to bed each night, I will . . .			
When it comes to rising earlier, I will . . .			
When it comes to prioritizing my day, I will . . .			
When it comes to multitasking, I will . . .			
When it comes to being prepared and engaged, I will . . .			
When it comes to minimizing distractions, I will . . .			

FIGURE 10.3 ■ The Stop, Start, and Keep of a Daily Masterpiece

Leader's Conversation Starter #2

Everyone deals with distractions, but only those seeking to be remarkable know how to track and eliminate the distractions that keep them from having the focus that is required to deliver remarkable performances. What distractions do you need to eliminate?

_____ Cell phone (calls, texts, e-mail)

_____ E-mail chimes (PC and phone)

_____ Social media alerts

_____ Instant messaging windows

_____ Cubicle drop-by visits

_____ Nonurgent, nonimportant tasks

_____ High-traffic areas

_____ Noises (music, loud talking, etc.)

_____ Other: _____

CHAPTER 11

What Just Happened Here?

Most of us plateau when we lose the tension between
where we are and where we ought to be.

—JOHN GARDINER

I F YOU have ever walked through a garden or other professionally planted environment during the winter months, you have probably seen plants, small trees, or bushes cut back to where, to the untrained eye, they look dead. It is almost enough sometimes to cause you to question what just happened here! It only takes a couple of minutes, however, with a professional gardener to learn that left to their own the plants would become a tangled and unorganized mess instead of the beautiful creation that we all love and admire. This process of pruning is performed to cut away the dead parts, the sick or dying parts, and even some healthy stems or blooms that might look good but are not the best.

Avoiding a Tangled Mess

If we use the example above as a metaphor, then the plants would represent your life, and you are the master gardener. The necessity for pruning is constant, and that job falls to you. If you want to reach your full potential, then you need to take on the intentional practice of pruning away the parts of your life that are dead or dying, and even some parts that may be producing good things but keep you from doing remarkable things.

Dr. Henry Cloud, in his book *Necessary Endings,* says that "growth depends on getting rid of the unwanted or the superfluous." In your life, just like that of the plants in the garden, you need to be on the lookout for things that take up your time and energy but that will never drive the results that you are looking for. For me this means deciding what I should be focusing on and letting other less important or nonproducing things go. You can never have a strong and lasting framework for remarkable if you do not prune away the things that occupy your time and attention but do not lead you closer to remarkable.

Better to be pruned to grow than cut up to burn.

—JOHN TRAPP

Just like the gardener, you need to make this process intentional and purposeful—meaning you must acknowledge the constant need for pruning and then do the pruning on a regular basis. There is a simple yet effective three-question approach to assessing what needs to be pruned in your life. These three questions will allow you to quickly assess and then take action to ensure you do not end up a tangled mess like the unpruned plant. You may also ask these three questions of a trusted friend or family member to get an outside perspective of where pruning may need to occur.

In the training that IBM leaders receive, they are taught these three questions as a simple way to evaluate their business and to enlist feedback from their team. Many leaders learn early that getting honest and productive feedback from your team on how you are doing can be challenging sometimes. People often hold back because they don't know how safe it is to share their thoughts about you with you. These three questions go a long way toward opening the door for open honest, safe communication.

The Three Questions of Pruning

Let's get the most important question out there first, *what should I stop doing?* Since most nonremarkable people struggle with saying no, this is a critical question for everyone desiring to deliver or lead remarkable performances. As we look at the framework in our Model for Remarkable, we see the building blocks of being exceptional, being disciplined, being prepared, and being persistent. Each one of these important building blocks can be weakened if we do not ask ourselves on a regular basis what we need to stop doing. If you hope to deliver and repeat your remarkable performances, you need to be aware of the things that take your time, money, energy, and resources but do not help you achieve the results you are looking to achieve.

One clear way to ensure that you know what to stop doing is to make sure that you have established a clear foundation layer for your

SAYING YES IMPLIES A NO

One of the great, yet painful, lessons I have learned over the years is that *saying yes to one thing means saying no to something else*. This may sound like a profoundly simple statement; yet it is a principle that almost everyone I know overlooks. I, of course, had to learn it the hard way by practically alienating my family. Because I am such a relationship-oriented person, I often go out of my way to help the people with whom I have the strongest relationships. This means *always* saying yes when they come to me looking for help or asking me to participate in something that is important to them. While I still desire to help and participate, I do so now only after consciously asking myself the following question:

If I say yes to doing _____ with _____ , what have I just said no to?

Then I list the things that I will *not* be able to do because I said yes to doing something else. For example, if a friend asks me to help him move some furniture on Saturday morning and I say yes, I have just said no to taking my wife to breakfast (a regular Saturday morning ritual). If I say yes to playing golf with my friends, I have just said no to preparing for that big speech tomorrow morning.

Saying yes is not the problem. Saying yes without considering what you just said no to is the problem. Make it a conscious choice, and you will find yourself on the road to remarkable.

Model for Remarkable. If you know your *what* and your *why,* making pruning decisions on what you should say no to becomes a whole lot easier.

One thing that leaders quickly learn at IBM is that there is no shortage of ideas for things we could be doing to drive more business. Remarkable businesses like IBM do remarkable things, and the temptation is to just keep doing more and more things, knowing that something is bound to work and drive the increased results. To be effective, however, and position ourselves for remarkable, and, more important, repeating remarkable, we ask our leaders to step back from time to time and give thought to this important question: What do we need to *stop* doing? The IBM business unit where the leader serves will provide the targets as well as the milestones for reaching those targets, but it is up to the leader to evaluate the dozens of tasks that are competing for his or her attention and determine what needs to be done and what needs to be stopped.

The second question of pruning is, *what should I keep doing?* This is a question that helps us to acknowledge where we see the greatest return on the investment of our time, money, energy, and resources. As I mentioned in the first question for pruning, many nonremarkable performers get caught in the trap of saying yes to everything that comes their way. The other side of that coin is to make clear decisions concerning what you should keep doing. Where are your greatest results found? What actions or tasks do you perform that truly add value to your customer or audience? These are clearly things you want to make sure that you have in your plan going forward and that you do with purpose and intentionality. By asking this question, you can shine a light on things that might now fall in the "what should I stop doing" bucket.

At IBM we have a process we run with our leaders after every quarter, called a root cause analysis, to determine whether we achieved our goals or not. The idea behind this exercise is that we achieved some positive outcomes and some negative outcomes and we would like to learn what kept the negative outcomes from becoming positive outcomes. This analysis uses the simple yet effective process of asking a series of why questions (you often hear this called the Five

Whys process, but if it takes more than five whys to get to the root, keep going). The idea is to take a look at a negative outcome and ask why it occurred. When you have an answer to that question, you ask why again. The asking of why continues until we are sure we are at the root of the problem and not trying to solve a symptom. Once you know you are at the root issue, you switch to problem-solving mode and brainstorm ways to correct the root problem.

Once a leader knows the cause of each effect, he or she can make adjustments and determine what we may need to stop doing, keep doing, or start doing to generate more of the positive outcomes and less of the negative. This is a key component in being able to drive and repeat remarkable results.

The third of the three questions of pruning is, *what should I start doing?* I made this the third question and not the first question on purpose. Starting new things can be easy to do. Most of us have an idea, and we move quickly to put that idea into place. But just as not every stem on a rose bush is good, not every new thing we start is good. Well, it may seem good, but it does not lead to great. It just becomes another thing we have to do. The essence of this question is to allow yourself to consider what you may be missing. The answer to this question of what to start may be personal development actions that help move you from good to great in the four areas of our framework for remarkable.

In any organization where you have highly engaged and highly intelligent individuals, you will have an abundance of new ideas and new things to try. This is definitely the case at IBM, where we pride ourselves on innovation and thinking outside the box. Innovation and out-of-the-box thinking are good and necessary things; however, doing new things just to be doing new things is a prescription for distraction if not handled properly. The way we equip our leaders to deal with the temptation of starting too many new things that may distract from what we are actually trying to accomplish is to insist they have a way to measure every set of new actions. This may seem incredibly obvious, but my experience has shown me that oftentimes leaders start new processes without knowing how they will determine if the process is working. If you do not have a metric or an indicator that will show clearly whether a new process is generating the desired result, then you should reevaluate the need for that new process. Average organizations are masters of doing a lot of things than have little or no impact on achieving the goals they have set.

If you are like me, starting new things is not a problem. I am an idea guy, and I have a thousand ideas of things I can start doing today. The problem, like the plants in the garden, is that more is not better. A combination of doing the right things and stopping the wrong things is what leads to productivity and success. It is so easy to spread yourself and your attention over so many seemingly good things that you miss the great things. Pruning can be difficult and even painful, but it is a short-term pain that, once endured, creates long-term gain.

Pruning IBM

I first learned of the concept of pruning when I watched IBM eliminate a division of the company where I had worked just a few short months earlier. As a matter of fact, the strong position of IBM in the marketplace today is a result of the actions the company took as a result of the answers to the three questions of pruning. When people or companies endeavor to assess where they are and what they need to stop, start, and keep doing, they can put themselves on the path to remarkable performances.

What IBM Needed to Stop Doing

IBM invented the personal computer business. And when I worked for the PC division in Raleigh, North Carolina, it was a vibrant and exciting place to work. But over time, markets began to shift, new technologies began to emerge, and what was once a thriving business began to show signs of fatigue. Oftentimes a company, just like an individual, will hold on to something for the simple reason that "we have always done it." This is a road map to a nonremarkable climate. IBM decided to sell the PC division even though the company was a pioneer in this important area of the information technology industry.

What IBM Needed to Start Doing

In one word—*services*. As times and economies were changing, IBM leadership saw the writing on the wall. Software and services would take the place of mainframes and PCs as the key revenue producers for the company. To jump-start the services area of the business, IBM purchased the consulting arm of PricewaterhouseCoopers. This put IBM on the map immediately and in a big way as a business and technology consulting company.

What IBM Needed to Keep Doing

Mainframes may have a shrinking market share, but they are not going away. IBM decided to keep doing mainframes and then add a strong middleware software component to drive increased customer value. In the software arena IBM decided to keep buying smaller companies that could provide the value our customers are looking for. And let's not overlook a key IBM focus from the earliest days of the company's founding—customer service. IBM will keep making a strong and positive customer experience a part of every decision that is made.

This constant analysis of what IBM should start, stop, and keep doing has given rise to remarkable performance during the trying times brought on by a global recession. And this analysis has also resulted in a fundamental change in how IBM goes to market. Just in the 10-year period between 2000 and 2010, the shift has been very noticeable. See Figure 11.1.

Help Me Prune Myself

It can be very difficult to prune yourself. Human nature seems to bless us all with an ability to see ourselves as being better than we really are. With that in mind, my suggestion is to seek the input of others when you analyze what you should start, stop, and keep doing. As I mentioned earlier, we encourage IBM leaders to use this start doing–stop doing–keep doing process when they want to get feedback from others.

Segment Profit Mix

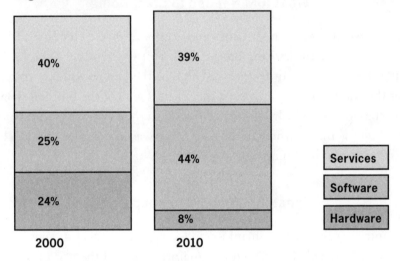

FIGURE 11.1 ▪ IBM's Changing Business Mix

http://www.the register.co.uk/2011/03/10/ibm_investor_day_2011_palmisano/

Often, though, when you ask those you work with for feedback on how you are doing, people will take the easy way out and just say, "You're doing great!" You may in fact be doing great, but most likely there are areas where you can improve. When you move away from directly asking for feedback and instead ask, "What should I stop doing that would help me be more effective in my role?" you will find that people are generally more open to providing ideas. It is a safer conversation for others to have with you, and it helps you to see past your blind spots.

I also use this approach with the members of my team to help them feel the freedom to provide me with valuable feedback. If you are a leader, you can get used to people telling you what you want to hear. It takes high trust developed over many months and even years to get to a point where the people who work for you will tell you the straight truth. To help speed this process along, I use the start, stop, keep questions to open the door and let them see that I am serious about hearing what they have to say. You can ask people to tell you how you can improve and hope they feel the courage to tell you the truth. Or you can ask, "What should I start doing that would really help our team to progress and improve?" or "What should I stop doing that gets in the way or does not add any value to our team performance?" When I first started doing this, all I would get from the members of the team was silence or some very polite, "Nothing, boss, you are doing all the right things." But after persisting with my questions, they began to see that I was serious about us growing as a team and me growing as a leader.

I also began to use this approach with customers. This was a little more painful because customers don't usually need a reason to tell you what you could do to improve. But once I began to open that door for them to share, the tone of the feedback changed and created an atmosphere that felt like we were all in this together and trying to grow and improve.

Pruning Is Not a One-Time Thing

When my wife prunes the roses and other plants and trees in our yard, she does not put away her pruning shears until next year. I will see her walking through the yard looking for anything that is out of place or not functioning as it should. The same is true for people who want to consistently deliver remarkable performances. There is big temptation to deliver a remarkable performance and think that I have arrived; I achieved it, and now I can just go with it. This will make repeating remarkable close to impossible. As my wife will tell you, beautiful roses require intentional effort. Weeds require nothing. Do nothing, and weeds will appear. It takes an intentional and meaningful effort to keep what is once remarkable, continuously remarkable.

CHAPTER 11 POWER POINTS

Many people miss remarkable because they are trying to do too many things or they are not doing the right things. In this chapter we looked into the importance of pruning and the effect it can have on your results.

The three questions to ask yourself and others when it comes to knowing how to improve your results are:

- What should I stop doing?
- What should I keep doing?
- What should I start doing?

Leader's Conversation Starter

This will sound easy, but it may take some coaching from you to get the desired result. If the members of the team do not trust your motives for asking, simply reassure them that—for you personally and the team corporately—to be remarkable you all need to ensure you are doing the right things. Have your team members answer the three key questions (stop, start, and keep) for the areas listed below and then discuss the answers openly with the entire team.

1. About you the leader (what should you stop, start, and keep doing):
   a. Stop: _____
   b. Start: _____
   c. Keep: _____

2. About the team members (what should they stop, start, and keep doing):
   a. Stop: _____
   b. Start: _____
   c. Keep: _____

3. About your customers (what should you and the team start, stop, and keep doing)
   a. Stop: _____
   b. Start: _____
   c. Keep: _____

PART III

The Functionality for Remarkable

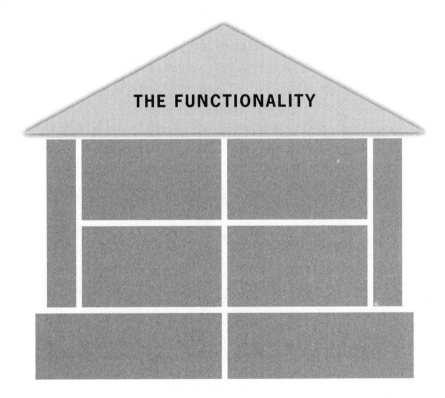

THE FUNCTIONALITY

The Model for Remarkable—Adding Function to Your Form

Character, in the long run, is the decisive factor in the life of an individual and of nations alike.

—THEODORE ROOSEVELT

ANOTHER COLLEGE football player has been asked to leave his team. This seems to happen more and more frequently these days. A star player with gifts and abilities that set him apart from others is derailed because of a violation of team rules or state laws. Another sports career that promised remarkable results is now thrown away and lost forever.

And, of course, this type of incident isn't exclusive to sports. It's not unusual to read about a political figure, charismatic and skilled in policy matters, throwing it all away because photos were released showing that he was not who he appeared to be. His reputation as a strong advocate for the people and someone you could trust to do the right thing was destroyed when his true character was revealed.

As we move into Part III of our Model for Remarkable, what I call the *functionality*, we will look into how important the components of excellence and character are to how remarkable appears to others. Much like our football player and politician, being skilled and capable doesn't mean a whole lot if your functionality doesn't align with your form.

As you recall in Part I, we established two building blocks of our foundation in the Model for Remarkable. Next, in Part II, we added the framework for our model and the four essential components required to ensure remarkable. Now, in Part III, we will discuss the final two components for a strong and lasting structure that will house every remarkable performance you ever deliver or lead.

Functionality Building Block #1:
Have a Mindset of Excellence

I call this final part of our model the functionality because these components will determine how you will function in the world around you. While the foundation and the framework of our model are incredibly important building blocks for everything remarkable, they are not seen by others. The functionality is where others experience the remarkable you (see Figure 12.1).

The first of the two components of the functionality is a *mindset of excellence*. Excellence is like the siding on your house—providing an attractive quality to the exterior that will differentiate you from others. Excellence is what your customers, prospects, friends, and strangers

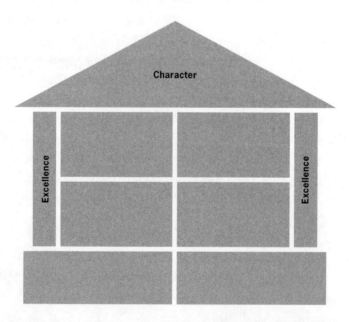

FIGURE 12.1 ▪ The Functionality of the Model for Remarkable

see when they encounter you. This is why it is the first building block of functionality.

As I mentioned earlier, when I ask the members of an audience if they would like to be average or excellent, they always tell me that they want to be excellent. But when we get down to looking at daily habits around how they actually do their work, it appears that it's easier to say the word *excellent* than it is to live in constant pursuit of excellence. Your desire to have customers, teammates, and family take notice of your performance will be lost if you do not make the choice of pursuing excellence in everything you do.

I have always thought that if you testify that you are a person of excellence, there had better be enough evidence to convict you. Too often it is all talk and not a lot of walk. People often say one thing and then do another. Perhaps I am not looking in the right places, but it seems that finding truly excellent work these days is a bigger challenge than it used to be. It seems that people in all areas of life are delivering just enough to get by. Cutting corners has become a sport,

A CLIMATE OF EXCELLENCE—LAUNCHING PAD FOR REMARKABLE

A mistake I often see people make when it comes to establishing a climate of excellence is that they think it is the responsibility of the company they work for to supply an environment of excellence. It would be great if your company did this, and many companies do, but you cannot sit around waiting for someone else to define excellence for you. Excellence is personal. Excellence is a mindset that you bring to everything you do. Excellence is required and is the launching pad for remarkable. Because excellence is our exterior siding in our model, it is what faces your audience, your customers. That means that excellence will be about personal service to others. It can be supported by the company climate, but you must define excellence for yourself and your team. And once you have done that, you can use your personal influence to begin to spread an attitude of excellence throughout the company where you work.

and settling for mediocrity has evolved into an acceptable way of life. Well, not for the remarkable! Remarkable people who lead remarkable performances don't settle for mediocrity; they do whatever it takes to do things right.

Does Remarkable = Excellence?

I am often asked the question of whether being remarkable simply means you are excellent at what you do. There is no way for people to be remarkable if they are not excellent at what they do. But being excellent is not enough to ensure being remarkable. Excellence is a prerequisite; but as our Model for Remarkable reveals, getting people to sit up and take notice or to remark on your performance takes something more.

Mike Holmes, from the *Holmes on Homes* television series that we spoke of earlier, knows the minimum building code, but he does not do his craft to the minimum building code. He does his best work so that it *exceeds* the expectations of the building code and the expectations of homeowners—and even that of the government authorities who do the inspections.

> *I want to take the word "minimum" out of the construction industry and stop the slow death of craftsmanship.*
> —MIKE HOLMES

We have all been the recipient of an excellent performance from someone or some company that left us feeling satisfied, although not impressed. For example, I fly a lot. Most days, I am served by airline employees who are excellent at doing their jobs; but they often stop well short of delivering what I would consider a remarkable performance. The best reason I can come up with why this happens is that they, like many of us, allow circumstance—like the weather, the price of gasoline, or the way others act toward us—to determine how they will do their jobs. I once asked a flight attendant who I thought was doing a remarkable job why his level of service was different from that of his coworkers on our flight. He admitted that he hated to see his colleagues do the "serve and hide." He explained that many of the attendants would do what was expected and then hide in the front or back of the plane until it was time for the flight to land. He told me that he had made the decision (there's that word again) to serve in such a way as to exceed expectations and make a customer take notice. That is excellence taken to the next level—remarkable!

So, remarkable requires excellence, but excellence alone isn't enough. We still need another building block to fully optimize the functionality of remarkable.

Functionality Building Block #2: High Character

Excellence is easy to achieve when things are going as planned. But when the storms come and the circumstances become difficult, *who you are* becomes an important component of what you can deliver. Having *high character* is our final building block and the component of our structure that will, like a roof on a house, protect us from the elements.

Note that all the building blocks throughout the three parts of the model are nothing unless they are driven by the character qualities of you as an individual. Without character, there will be nothing to keep you going when the storms hit—and everything you have built inside the house will be destroyed. Character serves as the roof over our heads, protecting all we do.

With character, not only can you master all the building blocks, but you can use them to construct and repeat a remarkable performance. Character should be the defining quality of a team or a company. It becomes who you are, and it is what your reputation is all about. These qualities will be the essence of any influence you have with your customers, colleagues, and companions. These qualities will also be a part of our continuing conversation in the chapters to come. Your performances can only be as remarkable as you are as a person. Your only chance to deliver repeatable remarkable performances is found in being the best you that you can be.

Be more concerned with your character than your reputation,
because your character is what you really are, while your
reputation is merely what others think you are.

—JOHN WOODEN

The Remarkable Me

When I think of character, I think of how someone responds to situations in his or her life. High-character people have something in them that allows them to respond in a positive and consistent manner no matter what the circumstances. My character predetermines my response, and my response determines the outcome. People who choose to *react* versus *respond* open the door for all kinds of character-destroying behaviors. Jim Rohn put it this way: "Character isn't something you were born with and can't change, like your fingerprints. It's something you must take responsibility for forming. You build character by how you respond to what happens in your life, whether it's winning every game, losing every game, getting rich or dealing with hard times."

One question that I am often asked when I speak about the role of character is whether someone without a strong character can deliver a remarkable performance. The answer is yes; if the conditions are right and the circumstances are favorable, a person of less than desirable character can deliver a remarkable performance. However, my experience as a leader of large teams is that if you ever hope to consistently repeat remarkable performances, you need a team of remarkable individuals. Remarkable individuals are people who are concerned about their character and how to be the best individual they can be. Remarkable individuals work on developing who they are so that they can deliver the outcomes and results that their customers desire.

One example that comes to mind is the fall from remarkable of Joe Paterno and the Penn State University college football program.

After a 45-year head coaching career and over 60 years at Penn State that were remarkable on many fronts, Coach Paterno will forever be linked to the child sex abuse scandal that rocked the university and the college football world. Whether the head coach is ever proved to have overlooked the abuse or not is irrelevant; his legacy will always be tarnished by what happened on his watch at the university. Before this was all uncovered, calling Joe Paterno and his record at the university remarkable was a common occurrence. Now, due to character failures on the part of many individuals, remarkable is not a word that can ever be used.

To review, here are the two building blocks in the functionality of remarkable performers:

1. Have a mindset of excellence.
2. Have high character.

Putting it all together, we now have the completed Model for Remarkable (see Figure 12.2).

FIGURE 12.2 ■ **The Model for Remarkable**

The IBM Way

In my years at IBM, there has always been a drive to provide remarkable performances for our customers. This drive is incorporated into an employee's belief system from the very first sales training classes that everyone must attend. The IBM basic beliefs when I joined the company were respect for the individual, customer service, and excellence. These principles were the heart of everything we did. I remember when I first joined the company as a rookie salesperson and I was placed in the care of the senior sales leaders. These senior sales leaders felt it was their role to initiate me into the fraternity of IBM selling; but they would never do anything that would get in the way of providing remarkable performances for our customers. The bar was set very high when it came to how we interacted with our customers. I recall more than once feeling that I would let down my team or disappoint my customers if I did not uphold my end of the relationship. My wife used to comment that it looked like I was in school again because I had homework every night. That was just me doing the preparation, exhibiting the dedication, and fine-tuning my focus so I could show up the next day ready to deliver a remarkable performance. I did not want to be the one to drop the ball or disappoint my team or my customers. This "climate of excellence" was how things were done and where I received my first introduction to what striving for remarkable means.

IBM founder Thomas J. Watson said, "If you want to achieve excellence, you can get there today. As of this second, quit doing less-than-excellent work." Excellence was part of his makeup, part of his basic belief system. He instilled it in his executive team and thus it was instilled in our corporate culture. IBM has been in existence for over 100 years, and that can be attributed to always remaining committed to serving our customers with excellence. There have been trying times and setbacks for sure, but remaining true to providing excellence in customer service can always help you to find you way back.

CHAPTER 12 POWER POINTS

Whether you are leading yourself or your team toward remarkable performances, you must take intentional, proactive steps to get there. If you allow yourself or your team to take the default path, you end up with average or worse. Remarkable requires intentionality.

In this chapter we have been looking at the functionality layer of our Model for Remarkable. The components of this model once again are:

- **The foundation.** Know the what and why of your goals.
- **The framework.** Be exceptional, be prepared, be disciplined, and be persistent.
- **The functionality.** Have a mindset of excellence and have high character.

To assist you in developing a strong functionality for leading yourself and your team, use these conversation starters to identify the places where you can grow and then decide on the actions to improve.

Leader's Conversation Starter #1

In Figure 12.3, determine if you exhibit the attribute or not by writing yes or no. Then on the right side, add a note about what you could do to improve in that particular area. If you are doing this with your team, allow all the team members to discuss two or three of their "no" items and what actions they plan to take. It is always good to hear the ideas of others when we are all trying to get to the same place.

Leader's Conversation Starter #2

Answer the following questions, paying careful attention to the evidence that would support your answers. This is a great activity for the people on your team to complete together as you address the components of delivering and repeating remarkable performances.

(*Note:* I know from personal experience that it is very easy to check off the questions with a "yes" in every blank. It takes little effort to talk

Y/N	Attributes	Actions
___	It is *never* "not my job"	___
___	I have a point of view	___
___	I share my point of view	___
___	I invite other points of view	___
___	I am creative	___
___	I am a problem solver	___
___	I am an encourager	___
___	I want the win, not the credit	___
___	I am authentic	___
___	I am optimistic	___
___	I am confident	___
___	I am humble	___
___	I invest in others	___
___	I help others improve	___
___	I question everything	___
___	I make things better	___
___	I have what it takes	___
___	I am a thought leader	___
___	I read books	___
___	I spend time thinking	___
___	I don't make excuses	___
___	I never blame others	___
___	I have a growth plan	___

FIGURE 12.3 ■ Personal Attributes of Remarkable Performers

of remarkable without actually doing the walk of remarkable. Behavior never lies. If you want to know how you are doing on the walk of remarkable, then look at your behaviors over the past months or the past projects. Use your behaviors as a guide for answering these questions.)

1. Do you truly desire to be remarkable in everything you do? _____
_____ .

How is that in evidence today? _____
_____ .

2. Are you willing to pay the cost of being remarkable? _____
_____ .

What cost have you paid to pursue remarkable? _____
_____ .

3. Are you willing to prepare, even when you don't know what you are preparing for? _____
_____ .

What preparation are you doing? _____
_____ .

4. Will you remain dedicated to the task at hand until it is completed in a remarkable way? _____
_____ .

5. Will you remain focused on the task at hand and put all that you are into its successful conclusion? _____
_____ .

What distractions will you need to address? _____
_____ .

6. Will you be persistent in getting things done in a remarkable way? _____
_____ .

How have you persisted in the past? _____
_____ .

7. Will you be tenacious, never quitting, especially when times are tough or setbacks occur? _____
_____ .

What is your biggest challenge when it comes to being tenacious?
_____
_____ .

CHAPTER 13

The Hall of Remarkable

I'll take any way to get into the Hall of Fame. If
they want a batboy, I'll go in as a batboy.
—PHIL RIZZUTO

I WAS WATCHING a sports broadcast on the induction of one of our
local sports heroes into the National Baseball Hall of Fame. As the
commentators on the broadcast presented this individual's career high-
lights and expounded upon why he deserved to be elected, you could
really get a sense for how remarkable his baseball career had been.
The combination of batting and fielding statistics generated over a
20-year career, as well as contributions to his community, made for a
story every baseball player longs for.

The Hall of Fame concept is not just unique to sports; many business and other nonsporting entities have a Hall of Fame for their area
of expertise. For anyone not familiar with the term, a *Hall of Fame* is
a type of museum established for any field of endeavor to honor individuals of noteworthy achievement in that field. In the case of professional sports, these halls of fame consist of actual halls or museums
that enshrine the honorees with sculptures, plaques, and displays of
memorabilia.[1] In each field that offers a Hall of Fame reward, there is a
set of measurements or accomplishments that are required for election
into the hall. This is something that is earned, not won.

Fame usually comes to those who are thinking about something else.
—OLIVER WENDELL HOLMES

I should note here that in all my research on reaching the Hall of Fame for both sports and business, I couldn't find any individuals who said that it was the overriding goal of their life to reach the Hall of Fame. To a person, they all said it was a "hope" or a "dream." Their goals were more firmly based on achieving remarkable results in their area of specialty and winning championships. People wanted to perform in such a way as to be worthy of Hall of Fame consideration, but receiving a vote for induction was out of their hands. The greatest thing they could do to provide an opportunity to be considered was to focus on being the very best they could be today. Be remarkable!

As we look deeper into the functionality layer of our Model for Remarkable, we will find that many of the characteristics of people who consistently provide remarkable performances are the same characteristics of Hall of Fame inductees.

Welcome to the Hall of Remarkable

If there were a Hall of Remarkable, what would it take for you to be considered for induction? I have already noted that it is the small, seemingly insignificant things done consistently over time that matter most, but what are some of those things?

What You Do Today Matters

The first is perhaps one of the single greatest lessons you can learn on this journey to providing remarkable performances: *what you do today matters*. As I have mentioned earlier in the book, the functionality layer of our Model for Remarkable is all about the things that people (customers, prospects, family, etc.) see in you. How you spend today tells people all they need to know about your ability to provide a remarkable performance. All remarkable performers recognize early and often the importance of how they invest today. They recognize that you cannot reap a harvest of success tomorrow if you are not willing to plant the seeds of discipline and hard work today. It is easy for us to watch a star ballplayer on game day and take note of what a remarkable athlete he is, but we easily disregard all the early mornings and late nights of disciplined hard work that no one sees that really made him great. Darren Hardy says, "Success is made one decision at a time." Hall of Remarkable performers make great decisions early and then execute those decisions daily, and over time these seemingly small decisions pay off with big results.

When training new employees at IBM, we continually remind them that it is the daily disciplines that lead to sustained success. Often new hires or employees who join IBM through acquisition struggle with the overwhelming size and intensity of the global organization. It becomes clear in a hurry that you need to first focus on what is important today in your area of responsibility. To worry about anything bigger than that is to take on things that can only frustrate and distract.

You Can't Be Remarkable Unless You Have Achieved Excellence

A second characteristic of Hall of Remarkable performers is their ability and desire to *be excellent*—mediocrity or average is not acceptable. This is a framework building block in our Model for Remarkable for a reason. As I've noted previously, excellence is not the same as remarkable, but being excellent at what you do is a major component of being remarkable. Hall of Remarkable performers pursue excellence in everything they do. From every workout to every meal, they have an understanding of what excellence looks like, and they never lose sight of it. This is as much about setting a goal and knowing what is required to attain that goal as it is anything else. Hall of Remarkable performers don't do average.

When I first joined IBM, I was struck by the focus on doing things in an excellent way. Over the years I have come to understand that this is a full-life concept, not a concept to be applied just at work. What I mean by that and what we teach every employee that comes through our doors is that you cannot just focus on being excellent during working hours and then live any way you want when you are away from work. Excellence is a mindset and cannot be turned on and off. Either you are a person of excellence, or you are not. We spoke earlier of the importance of how you lead yourself when it comes to being a remarkable performer; well, being a person of excellence is a key component of how you lead yourself, and it carries over into everything you do.

Passion Drives Performance

Another key characteristic of Hall of Remarkable performers is their *passion* for what they do. Many of us do what we do because it pays the bills or because we are making someone else happy by doing it, not because we have a gift and a passion for doing it. Michael Jordan really liked baseball. He even had above-average skills at playing the game. But Michael Jordan had a *passion* for playing basketball. He was obviously gifted at basketball, and when he matched his passion with his gift, not only did he become arguably one of the best basketball players of all time, but he achieved Hall of Fame credentials. Why do you do what you do? Are you passionate about it, and do you utilize your natural gift? You will always struggle to achieve Hall of Remarkable results if you are not working in the area of giftedness and passion.

Because IBM is a customer-facing organization, its employees think a lot about passion and how it shows in their day-to-day work efforts. It is easy to allow circumstances and the normal ups and downs of daily work life to control how you feel or what others sense when they are around you. People who are passionate about what they do have a built-in mechanism to overcome these challenges and instead consistently communicate a positive and upbeat demeanor. One question I often ask leaders at IBM when talking about passion is to tell me what cause they are fighting for. If they tell me they are fighting to achieve their quota, I know immediately we have a passion problem. If they tell me they are fighting to help solve customer problems and help make the world a better place through IBM solutions and technology, I know they have established a launching pad for a remarkable performance.

Continual Development Is Essential for Growth

A fourth characteristic found in Hall of Remarkable performers is a commitment to a lifetime of *continual development*. When I looked at sports and business Hall of Fame performers, I found that they each had an attitude of always learning and growing in their craft. They never thought that they had arrived, that they had come as far as they could in their specialty area. When they won a championship, they returned the next season to training camp and worked hard on the fundamentals. Hall of Remarkable performers are never satisfied with their accomplishments, even if those accomplishments are remarkable. Remarkable performers are always setting new goals and driving hard to attain them. They never stop the process of growing and learning.

Personal development and professional development are the hallmark of what makes IBM a remarkable place to work. Employees are not only encouraged but mandated to develop their skills in various ways throughout the year. From classrooms to online sessions and from one-on-one coaching to book clubs, all IBMers are required to stay on top of their skill development and take the actions necessary to acquire the skills they need to be the very best they can be. A key part of our annual performance review is a recap of what personal development actions individuals took during the previous years and what actions they will take in the year to come.

Expressing Gratitude Recognizes That Others Have Provided Support

And finally, every Hall of Remarkable performer must exhibit the character quality of *gratefulness*. As I reviewed various Hall of Fame presentations and celebrations from over the years, I noticed that every single inductee acknowledged the help he or she received from others to achieve this great accomplishment. The inductee would express appreciation for the help and support not only of teammates and coaches, but also of spouses and loved ones who made sacrifices so that this person could succeed. No one gets to the Hall of Remarkable without such help. Be grateful and recognize those in your life that make it possible for you to do what you do.

While the word *gratefulness* is not often used in a corporate environment, I think that it is at the heart of what remarkable performers know that average performers may not grasp. Let me underscore again this important point: no one makes it in this environment without a lot of help from others. Teamwork is the essence of the remarkable results that IBM has experienced. With ever-increasing complexity in the technology market, it is impossible for just one person to solve a client's requirement. It takes a team of trained professionals to deliver our very best, and strong teams are made up of grateful people—grateful for their teammates and grateful for how they can work together to solve complex customer issues.

American football player Dan Fouts said, "You strive to win a Super Bowl and you do everything you can to get there. But being in the Hall of Fame, you never play for that honor. It's incredible." Being in any Hall of Fame is indeed a great honor, and it is something that is earned over many years of repeatable, remarkable performances. To be considered for the Hall of Remarkable, you have to develop a daily

THE TWO PAINS

Jim Rohn once said, "We must all suffer from one of two pains: the pain of discipline or the pain of regret. The difference is discipline weighs ounces while regret weighs tons."

The truth in this statement is evident to all of us who did not take the steps we knew we needed to take for fear of the pain it would cause, only to reap the regrettable consequence at a later time. The pain of discipline is easily forgotten when the victory is won. The pain of regret endures forever.

Developing the strength of discipline in your life means focusing more on the long-term results than on the short-term pain or cost. You will always reap what you sow; thus you should be intentional with when and how you sow the seeds of your remarkable future.

commitment and discipline to do the things and take the actions that will put you in the position for this kind of honor. You cannot simply earn some early success and then back off or begin to take it easy. Performers who do that never make it to the Hall of Remarkable.

Ever Onward

To be consistently remarkable in all that you do, you must always be pushing forward. The best way I have found to do this is to adapt an approach to life and work that I learned from watching my two nephews become U.S. Marines.

Over a span of a year and a half, I had the great honor and pleasure to visit the training facilities of the U.S. Marines at Parris Island, South Carolina, and Quantico, Virginia. I was there to witness the graduations of my nephews Tyler and Stephen as they became U.S. Marines. The pride I experienced is almost indescribable; the lessons I learned are invaluable.

There is no room in any military action for average or mediocre performance. All the troops—every man and woman involved in the action—must be at the top of their game, and they must be in a position to provide remarkable results. When I look at the way many performances are derailed due to either complacency or the failure to push forward, I know we all can learn from how the military ensures that remarkable is consistent and repeated.

Lessons in Remarkable from IBM and the U.S. Marines

While I was noting the lessons from the training of the U.S. Marines, I realized that these very same lessons are what we are teaching our leaders at IBM. The first and most important quality that every Marine and every leader must learn upon arriving for the first day on the job is *personal discipline.* I have already discussed the importance of personal discipline, so let me just add here that no matter how you feel today, no matter what else is going on in your life, no matter how tired you may be, you just do it. When I think of all the excuses I have come up with over the years to *not* do the thing that needed to be done when it needed to be done, I wonder how I was able to get anything done. Remarkable comes to the person who is able to remain disciplined and get things done, no matter the circumstances or challenges.

Some people spend an entire lifetime wondering if they made a difference in the world. But, the Marines don't have that problem.
—RONALD REAGAN

A second characteristic that the Marines exhibited and that we teach our IBM leaders is to always *be prepared*. You might be wondering why I keep coming back to this concept of being prepared, but if you had seen as many performances as I have that went up in smoke due to lack of preparation, you would harp on it too. The truth I learned from the Marine training that I almost never see in business training is that being prepared also means anticipating all the possible circumstances that might arise and then ensuring you have a response for each situation. One way we reinforce this concept to our leaders at IBM is by asking them to adapt a coaching mindset with each of their direct reports. The coaching mindset allows the senior leader to ask the junior leader "what-if" types of questions. By taking the time to think through each possible scenario and then decide on a course of preparation and action should that scenario occur, leaders build the confidence to know that they can accomplish anything. The Marines know, as we all should, that when an opportunity presents itself, it is too late at that point to plan a response; you have to have already anticipated that opportunity or situation and have prepared for it accordingly. You never know what, or when, opportunity will knock, so always be prepared.

Another notable characteristic of Marines becomes obvious almost immediately. You can't watch a Marine training exercise for more than a minute without seeing the importance of *teamwork*—you never see a Marine alone. The soldiers are always moving about in teams or squads. They are trained to work as one and communicate continually. This is a constant struggle in a large, multinational organization like IBM. Everyone will tout the importance of teamwork, but sometimes it is just easier to do things yourself. The problem in the corporate world, like the military world, is that there is just too much to do, and you cannot repeat remarkable performance if you are always going it alone. When I asked my nephews about this teamwork aspect, they both commented that being in a team environment had several advantages. One, you work harder so you don't let your partner or your squad down. Two, you work longer because there is always a teammate there to come along side you and help you through the challenging times. For remarkable performers, it can be very tempting to go it alone, but as I explained earlier when speaking about gratefulness, there is no alone. You may feel alone during the performance, but there is always someone who has been there for you and encouraged you to go harder or go longer than you thought you could.

Marines are trained from the very beginning to never stop until the job is done. There is no halfway; there is no shortcut. For the remarkable performer this is the skill of *follow-through*. My wife will tell you that for a time in the early years of our marriages, I would start a project around the house and then drift away to something else, because I either didn't have a part that I needed or didn't know what to do next. The unfinished project would then lie on the workbench cluttering up my work space and keeping me from starting another project. I have since learned the importance of following through and completing what I start in every aspect of my life. Many leaders suffer from this same condition. They run into a roadblock, or they need to contact another group for some additional information, and the work effort gets pushed to the side. Our customers tell us that the quickest way for an IBM salesperson to lose credibility is to not follow through on the things he or she promised to do. There is no possibility of achieving a remarkable performance if you do not follow through and complete what you start. If you tell people you will do something, then do it; or come back to them and tell them why you can't do it. Never leave something undone.

Vigilance in Remaining Remarkable

As my day with my nephews came to a close, I found one other quality of a U.S. Marine that caused me to pause and think of how important it is to delivering a remarkable performance, the quality of *vigilance*. The Marines are always standing guard, watching over their mission, and ensuring that nothing unwanted creeps in to undo the remarkable work they have done. For civilians like you and me, I think this translates into keeping watch over our work and over ourselves. Keeping watch over our work means to ensure that what we have done stands the test of time and delivers the value we committed it would provide. Keeping watch over ourselves means to ensure that we do not allow our remarkable success to cause us to embrace complacency or stop pushing forward toward our goal.

After spending time with the men and women of the U.S. Marines, I am more convinced than ever that having a strong functionality layer in our Model for Remarkable means making good choices and doing the things that make remarkable possible. We have learned these exact same principles in the training of our leaders at IBM. You must be intentional. You must be diligent. It is too easy to lie back and rest on your past successes. You may have been remarkable once, but you will never repeat remarkable without making these important, intentional choices to live your life differently.

CHAPTER 13 POWER POINTS

In this chapter we explored the characteristics of someone you might find in the Hall of Remarkable, if there were such a place. As part of the functionality layer of our Model for Remarkable, these are the qualities others will see and use to determine if you are capable of delivering a remarkable performance. These qualities include:

- Being disciplined
- Being prepared

- Being a team player
- Following through
- Being vigilant

Leader's Conversation Starter

Look at Figure 13.1 with your team and then have each person evaluate the team against the five qualities for keeping focused on remarkable. At the bottom of the figure, there is a place for team members to capture actions that the team could take to improve the chances for remarkable performances. Use the team's responses as a discussion guide to help keep every individual focused on what must be done to position the individual and the team for being remarkable.

How disciplined are we today?	→	Very ... Sort of ... Not Very
How prepared are we today?	→	Very ... Sort of ... Not Very
How strong is our teamwork today?	→	Very ... Sort of ... Not Very
How strong is our follow-through with our customers and ourselves?	→	Very ... Sort of ... Not Very
How strong is our vigilance in keeping our team focused on remarkable?	→	Very ... Sort of ... Not Very

1. _____

2. _____

3. _____

FIGURE 13.1 ▪ Remarkable Qualities Evaluation

CHAPTER 14

Staying the Course Even After Success

Success is a lousy teacher. It seduces smart people into thinking they can't lose.

—BILL GATES

As a young boy, I had the privilege and the pleasure of living on the Space Coast of Florida. My father was an engineer with the space program, and I was able to see every manned space launch through the Mercury, Gemini, and Apollo programs. I didn't think it was a privilege at the time, but the older I get, the more I see that time as every child's dream. I mean, what child wouldn't love to watch rockets soaring over his house?

Let's work the problem, people. Let's not make things any worse by guessing.

—GENE KRANZ

When you think of the U.S. space program and all that was accomplished, it is easy to attach the word *remarkable*. As an IBMer, I take even more pride in the space program accomplishments knowing how involved IBM was in that program. There is plenty of success there to cause one to sit up and take notice. The men and women of NASA, along with their partners at IBM and the other space agencies, made the remarkable look easy, but of course it was not. And it was not all glamour and reward; there have been tragedies and setbacks along the way. These tragedies and setbacks served as reminders to all involved that they should never become complacent or take for granted that just because they put a rocket into space last month, that they could do it again this month.

The Successful Failure

I recall during the flight of *Apollo 13*, the failed attempt to reach the moon, how the TV networks decided not to carry the broadcasts from the space capsule just prior to the scheduled landing on the moon. It was like going to the moon had all of a sudden become so boring that no one would watch the broadcast. Because my dad was a part of the space program and we lived it every day, we would be glued to the TV

A ONE-DEGREE CHANGE OF COURSE

When an individual or a corporation experiences success, there is a tendency to stop doing some of the things that led to that success. Some tasks just don't seem necessary any longer. This complacency can cause a change in course that is usually undetectable in the short term. Unfortunately, as time goes by, the deviation from the desired course becomes more and more obvious.

If an airplane leaves San Diego, California, headed for New York City and the heading is only off by one degree, the result will be that the plane misses New York City completely. The longer you fly, the more off course you will be.

Fight the urge to back off after a great success. Instead challenge yourself and your team to:

- Increase expectations of what should be delivered next
- Increase engagement of all the people involved
- Increase positive attitude training
- Make midcourse corrections when needed

for these types of broadcasts. Plus, three astronauts doing a live TV show just a few miles from the moon is a pretty cool thing to watch when you are a kid. Of course, immediately after the "nonbroadcast" ended, there was an explosion on board the spacecraft, and a weeklong struggle was under way to bring the astronauts home safely. We were all glued to our television sets now.

When we talk about the Model for Remarkable and the layer of functionality, we need to consider a key challenge of delivering and repeating remarkable performances—staying the course even after you have been successful. For some reason we have a tendency, if left to our default mechanism, to alter our course after having a good success in our life. We either stop doing something we had been doing or ignore warning signs that we would never have ignored before the success. The reason for this can be as simple as getting lazy once success has been won, or the reason might be more complex like the failure to understand or appreciate the amount of work and dedication that went into the victory. Sometimes the path to success can become so routine that we lose our focus on what we are really trying to accomplish. I recall reading about a news reporter asking *Apollo 13* commander Jim Lovell if it bothered him that the public regards this flight as routine. Lovell's response was that there was nothing routine about flying to the moon. When remarkable becomes routine, then there is going to be difficulty in repeating that remarkable performance. Whatever the reason, suffice it to say that you cannot deliver the two building blocks of the functionality layer—excellence and high character—unless you diligently stay the course that can lead you to remarkable.

When the New Wears Off

Think back to when you started a new job or joined a new club or perhaps when you started at a new school when you were younger. Do you recall the energy and excitement of those early days in your new adventure? And do you remember how, over time, that feeling of energy and excitement began to slowly disappear? Why is that? Does it always go away? Does it have to go away? Can you keep it from going away?

When I speak with leaders about this phenomenon of disappearing energy, we often compile a list of the reasons why we think people back off their initial high-energy ways after they begin to be successful. I am sure that what we have come up with is not a complete list, but it helps to provide a good idea of the challenges that leaders face when they want to ensure that remarkable performance occurs and is repeated on a regular basis. Here are some of the reasons we identified:

- The team gets comfortable with the work.
- The team figures out the minimum requirement to get by.
- The initial challenge goes away, and there are no new challenges.
- The team doesn't feel like what it does matters.
- The team doesn't feel like it is making progress.
- The team doesn't know how it is doing.

This is true for all of us—when we start something new, there is always an energy and excitement. There are a lot of new challenges and new experiences to be enjoyed. But over time, routine sets in, and the challenge fades. This feeling of fading challenges causes people to disengage from their work. Their hands may still be involved, but you have lost their heart and their head. Once this happens, remarkable will become very difficult to achieve, if not impossible.

A Daily Dose of Energy and Excitement

If you are like most people, then you have been trained to expect the energy and excitement level of doing a job to decrease the longer you do that job. But "most people" are *not* remarkable performers. If you really want to differentiate yourself in today's workplace, then you need to devise a new way of approaching what you do. This becomes even more important once you and your team have experienced some sort of success, since it is after you experience success that routine can set in and the attitudes and actions of mediocrity develop momentum.

By far, the greatest attribute I have seen in individuals and teams who are able to repeat remarkable performances can be wrapped up in the word *attitude*. If you are like a lot of people, you probably just gave out a short sigh indicating a "here we go again with the attitude discussion." That can be a common response until you learn the power that attitude has in the life of a remarkable performer. I learned this important fact when a friend decided to start his own business with the sole purpose of providing attitude training. I laughed and encouraged him to add some other options to the menu. He laughed back and said, "Why would I want to do that? Attitude is everything." What he knew then and I know now is that he was right—attitude *is* everything, and his business was a huge success. After leading dozens of teams over the years, I would much rather be surrounded by people with great attitudes who need help developing their skills than I would skilled people with lousy attitudes. You can teach skills, but attitude is a choice.

Attitude Is Everything

As part of the leadership training we provide at IBM, we speak a lot about the attitude you bring to every project, event, or interaction. Whether you hold the title of a leader or not, people are watching. We often point out that the attitude display will be the attitude you get back from the people you are working with. If you have a negative approach to what must be done, then more than likely the team will take a negative approach.

I recall hearing author and speaker Zig Ziglar tell a story about being at an airport and preparing to travel home after a long road trip. Just before he was to board his flight, the gate agent made an announcement that the flight was being canceled. While almost everyone else seated in the boarding area began to get angry and complain, Mr. Ziglar exclaimed, "Fantastic!" When the gate agent asked him what was so fantastic, he told her that he realized that airlines only cancel flights for one of three reasons. One, the plane is broken; two, there is something wrong with the pilot; or three, the weather is dangerous. He then explained that if any of those were true today, then he would prefer not to fly, and the fact that the airline had made that decision for him was "Fantastic!" The difference between

Mr. Ziglar and the majority of the other people in the gate area was the attitude they each displayed at the circumstance that had been presented to them.

The people there had a choice to make concerning how they would view this situation and how they would respond. The problem with "most people" is that they choose to *react* versus respond. Mr. Ziglar made the choice to respond in this situation, and it differentiated him from the other passengers. Ever since I told my family this story, we have begun to use this "fantastic approach" with many of the challenges we face. We were in a restaurant and the server was ignoring us, and when I questioned him to ask why, he explained that there was a large group of people at another table and he felt they needed more of his attention than we did. As my face began to redden, my wife leaned over and said, "Isn't that *fantastic!*" We all had a smile and immediately made the choice to respond rather than react.

The Two Mindsets

As we remind our IBM leaders as they are preparing to lead their teams, the choice of responding versus reacting is a skill that all remarkable performers must master. But an even more important skill necessary to be able to repeat remarkable is the ability to recognize the two mindsets of attitude. This may sound so simple that you will skip over it in search for something meatier, but let me warn you: this seemingly insignificant act will make or break every performance you ever give. The two mindsets look like this:

Mindset #1: I have to do this. This is usually expressed this way: "I have to do this report." "I have to go to my parents' house." "I have to go on a sales call." "I have to go to my child's piano recital." This mindset sends you into your task with an underlying attitude of just getting it over with: "Oh please just let me survive and move on to something else. I cannot wait until this is over."

Mindset #2: I get to do this. This is usually expressed like this: "I get to drive my brother to the mall." "I get to start a new project at work." "I get to take my son to baseball practice." This mindset sends you into your task with an underlying attitude that this is the opportunity of a lifetime. "I can't wait to get on that stage [or join my team, or be with my family, etc.] and encourage this audience [whether it is 1 or 1,000]."

The choice you have made about mindset is communicated not only by your words but also by the nonverbal signals that you give off. When you have an "I have to" mindset, your voice is low, your shoulders are slumped, and your eyes are cast down. When you have an "I get to" mindset, your words are upbeat, your head is held high, and your eyes are gleaming. My point in telling you this is that people know what mindset you brought with you whether you tell them or not.

I had this all pointed out to me some years ago when a friend heard me say, "I have to go to my daughter's piano recital." He stopped me right then and asked if I really meant what I just said. I said, "Yes, I *have* to go." He asked, "Don't you mean you *get* to go?" It was at that moment that I became aware of the choice I was making and the

WHAT COMES OUT WHEN YOU ARE SQUEEZED?

Can you really change your attitude? That might seem like a silly question, but many people act as if their attitude was something they were born with and they have no choice in the matter.

Your attitude is displayed when some stimulus occurs and you are being squeezed. What comes out when you are squeezed is directly related to what is in you. Squeeze a grape, and you get juice. Squeeze you, and you get what's in your heart and mind.

If you want positive to come out when you are squeezed, then you will need to work on putting positive in. You do this by:

- Reading, listening, and watching positive content
- Spending time with positive, upbeat people
- Reading and studying books on developing a positive attitude

message I was communicating through every event on my calendar. I quickly made the commitment that I would make the choice to be an "I get to" kind of guy.

Choosing your mindset is an intentional act, and it will have consequences. Mindset #1 leads to fear, uncertainty, and doubt. Your focus is on *you,* and you are worried mainly about surviving. It always leads to an inferior performance. That performance might be in front of a customer or in front of your spouse or children. It might be in front of your class or in front of your parents. The size of the audience does not matter; your choice of mindsets is what will matter.

Mindset #2 leads to strength, certainty, and presence. The focus is on those you are serving and how you can add value to their lives in these precious few minutes you have with them. Whether you are serving 1 or 1,000, choosing an "others-oriented" approach and an "I *get to*" mindset will establish an energy in you that will carry through the toughest of assignments.

Does choosing Mindset #2 mean you won't have fear, uncertainty, or doubt? Of course not, but it does mean that you can take any of those feelings and redirect them into a positive energy that both you and your customers can use for good.

Great Expectations

Another way that individuals and corporations stay the course even after having a lot of success is to continue to increase expectations of what is required. At IBM, one of the reasons that we faced bankruptcy in the early 1990s was that complacency had set in after years of having a highly successful business. Expectations were for more of the same. What got us here was good enough to get us where we wanted to go. That is a quick recipe for a failing performance. If you leave the bar where it was previously set, human nature will find a way to get just barely over it. If you raise the bar and increase the level of expectations, then you will be forced to raise the level of performance required to achieve the new expectations. When IBM began to make its comeback in the mid-1990s, its turnaround was directly related to a change in leadership and an increase in what that new leader said was expected from each of us going forward.

Something else warrants comment here about those challenging years when IBM was trying to rebound—the role that *humility* plays in delivering a remarkable performance. In those early years when IBM was setting new revenue and profit records, it was common for the press to write about the company's arrogance. IBM was making and exceeding all the numbers, and it really did not much care about what anyone else thought of it. As the 1990s progressed and things got bad, the arrogance began to fade. And as the company began to rebuild, a sense of humility, at least in the areas where I was working, began to emerge. Up until this point in our history, it was unthinkable that IBM could be approaching bankruptcy. It was unthinkable that IBM would have to lay off thousands of workers, but it did. With the new leadership and a new expectation of performance, IBM began to put the pieces back together, but this time with an entirely new outlook. Once you experience the pain of setback and defeat, you begin to realize that having years of sustainable success is no guarantee of future years of sustainable success. The minute you start to think otherwise is the minute you have put yourself in a position to fail.

> *High achievement always takes place in the framework of high expectation.*
> **—CHARLES KETTERING**

The great lesson for those individuals and companies desiring to deliver remarkable performances is that *expectations need to always be increasing and humility needs to always be present.* If you back off on the expectations and push forward on the pride of having arrived, you have just signed yourself or your organization up for a very tumultuous future.

Engagement Factors

Another area to consider if you hope to continue driving remarkable performance is employee engagement. Your personal level of engagement or the engagement level of your team will determine the level of performance you will be able to achieve. By *engagement* I mean the extent to which you are emotionally connected and have bought in to the work you are doing. I have a simple but effective way of gauging where I am personally, or where my team is, when it comes to engagement, and that is to look for signs of ownership or signs of observership. By this I mean, do I feel like I own the business or the project, or am I just observing the business or project? Owners engage and connect to the business or project in completely different ways than observers do. Owners take it personally. Observers can take it or leave it. Owners feel responsible for the outcomes. Observers take whatever outcomes develop. Owners change course when conditions dictate. Observers change course when they are told to change course, and then they complain about it to others. Owners are positioned precisely where a remarkable performance will occur. Observers will not deliver remarkable performances.

When training IBM leaders who manage large (or even small) teams of people, we spend a lot of time looking at how they can monitor and increase the engagement level of their team. We teach that the greater the engagement level, the greater the performance of the team or individual. When individuals disengage, 9 times out of 10 it has to do with the manager the person works for. Increasing engagement of individuals on your team can be accomplished by doing many of the things we are discussing in this book—things like:

- Establishing one-on-one communication with each individual on your team
- Communicating clearly your expectations for every member of your team
- Reminding individuals on your team of why the team needs them in their role

- Expressing appreciation to every individual for his or her contribution to the team
- Expressing to every member of the team that he or she is valued

When we send managers out to manage a team at IBM, they have been warned that people don't quit a company; they quit a person. Don't be that person!

The Engagement Test

Take a moment to read through the engagement assessment in Figure 14.1. While a simple exercise, I think you will see the difference between someone who is engaged and emotionally connected to what he or she does and someone who is simply an observer. Put a check mark next to the statements that describe you. The power of this exercise is in its ability to make you aware of where you stand. Many times it is knowing the truth about where you stand that opens the door to making the necessary changes to increase performance and position yourself for remarkable results.

The Engagement Test

Owner	Observer
_____ I think about the project I am working on when I'm not at work.	_____ I seldom think about the project I am working on when I'm not at work.
_____ Time seems to fly when I am at work.	_____ I cannot wait for five o'clock to get here when I am working.
_____ I love to tell others what I do and what I am working on.	_____ I never tell others what I do and what I am working on.
_____ It hurts me when others think my work is irrelevant.	_____ I could care less what others think about the work I do.

FIGURE 14.1 ▪ Owners or Observers?

It goes without saying that no company, small or large, can win over the long run without energized employees who believe in the mission and understand how to achieve it.

—JACK WELCH

CHAPTER 14 **POWER POINTS**

Having a strong functionality layer in our Model for Remarkable means you must stay the course after you have enjoyed success. This seems like it would be an easy thing to do, but because of our natural tendencies to back off or slow down, it's not. In this chapter we learned some of the reasons why this is so and what you can do to avoid the natural desire to change course. The key learning points we covered are:

- **Your attitude matters.** Which of the two attitude mindsets are you choosing? Do you have the "I get to" mindset, or do you default to the "I have to" mindset?
- **Increasing your expectations is a necessity.** If you don't hold yourself to a higher standard, then no one else will. Decide on what's next and then set your expectations on that new goal.
- **High engagement will raise the level of performance for yourself and your team.** After success, it is easy to disengage. We talked about developing an "owner" mentality versus an "observer" mentality.

Leader's Conversation Starter

Ask the people on your team to answer the following questions on their own and then have them share their answers with the group. This is a great way to uncover some of the thoughts and feelings that often undermine your best intentions to stay the course. If you do not have a team, you may answer these questions for yourself.

1. What is our greatest strength as a team? To what do you attribute our success?_____

_____

_____

2. What is our greatest obstacle to growing our success?_____

_____

_____

3. What actions should we take to increase our ability to deliver another remarkable performance?_____

_____

_____

CHAPTER 15

Inspire Me Toward Remarkable

If your actions inspire others to dream more, learn more,
do more and become more, you are a leader.

—JOHN QUINCY ADAMS

I CAME ACROSS a CNN Money article[1] about a survey of workers conducted by Mercer Consulting. The consulting firm discovered that over 50 percent of workers were so unhappy with their jobs and their companies that they were considering leaving the company. How can you ever hope to deliver remarkable products or service to your clients if one-half of your team is thinking about jumping ship? It's not possible. So what's a leader to do? *Answer:* Inspire your team!

Life is a people business. If you want to do well in life, you need to learn early how to get along well with others. When it comes to being in business and leading a team to drive business results, it is imperative that you do more than just get along well with others. Great leaders know how to inspire others, and when people are inspired, they can be remarkable. Author and speaker Jack Zenger, in his book *The Inspiring Leader: Unlocking the Secrets of How Extraordinary Leaders Motivate,*[2] says, "As a leader of an organization, you are the role model, and people are watching you 24/7; you are never offstage. If you want the organization to be responsive to customers, you have to be responsive to customers. If you want your people to maintain good working hours, you need to maintain good working hours." As we spoke about earlier, people do what people see.

As we continue in this section about the functionality in our Model for Remarkable, I think it is important to address the topic of being an inspiring leader. You may say, "But I am not a leader!" That doesn't excuse you from being inspiring to others. Leadership is about your

PASSION INSPIRES

Author and speaker Suze Orman once said, "You cannot inspire unless you are inspired yourself." Where does your inspiration come from? What are you passionate about?

I once read about a consultant who asked a group of people to list their three favorite movies. Once they had listed the three movies, she asked them why these movies were favorites. When the people began to explain what they loved about a particular movie, you could see that it sparked some sort of passion inside them. Something in the storyline or in the lead characters resonated with the individual.

I tried this for myself and found that I am drawn to movies about people who prevail after overcoming some sort of setback or injustice. I lean toward stories where people persevere and take the difficult steps necessary to succeed. I especially feel an empathy with the role of the encourager in the movie—that one person who believes that the other characters have what it takes to succeed. My conclusion: I am passionate about encouraging others and helping people grow.

What would your evaluation say about your passions? What type of characters are you drawn to?

- The lead characters that tell the story and show the way?
- The colead characters that challenge the lead and help overcome challenges?
- The support characters that provide data and insight for the story?
- The support characters that provide physical and emotional support for the lead?

No matter your passion, find it and use it to inspire others toward remarkable!

ability to positively influence others. You do not need the title of leader to do that. The ability to inspire others toward remarkable performance is a very visible thing, and that is why it is a key ingredient in the functionality of our model and why it is essential to achieving excellence and having high character.

The Law of the Picture at IBM

When I think of "people do what people see," I am reminded of the recovery from near bankruptcy that IBM embarked on in the 1990s. New CEO Louis Gerstner began immediately to emulate exactly what he wanted all of us at IBM to do—embrace our customers. While Wall Street was asking Mr. Gerstner for a strategy and a recovery plan, he was going door-to-door to see IBM customers worldwide. He called it Operation Bear Hug, and he asked every customer-facing IBM employee to do the same. He took some heat from Wall Street when he said that the last thing IBM needed at the moment was a strategy, but time has proved he was right. Many leaders tell their people what to do, but that is not leading; that is managing. True leaders don't say go and do; they say *let's* go and do.

An Example of Inspiring Leadership—Nelson Mandela

I was invited to give some leadership talks in Johannesburg, South Africa. It was to be my first visit to South Africa, and I looked forward to learning a bit of the history of this great country. In the months leading up to my visit, there was a lot of news coming out of South Africa. The Soccer World Cup was being held there, and the Hollywood movie *Invictus* was enjoying success at the box office. Even with all that great coverage, I cannot think of South Africa without thinking of Nelson Mandela. During my visit I was able to spend some time looking at his life and the impact this one man has had on the development of a country. The stories of his leadership style and the influence he has had are inspiring, to say the very least. To learn that he spent 27 years in prison before leading the nation to where it is today makes the story even more remarkable.

Leadership Lessons That Inspire

One of the first things you will notice in the story of Nelson Mandela is the *courage* he displayed in the face of incredible challenges and setbacks. Mandela said, "I learned that courage was not the absence of fear, but the triumph over it. The brave man is not he who does not feel afraid, but he who conquers that fear." The lesson for leaders who desire to inspire their teams is that fear is not the problem; giving into fear is the problem. Mandela said he felt fear many times, but he refused to give into it. He knew that others were watching him, and he wanted his courage to be inspirational. Moving beyond fear is what inspiring leaders do.

When training leaders at IBM, we don't normally use the word *courage*, but maybe we should. Courage is not a word that most people associate with leading a team, but we do talk about overcoming the natural fears that come with leadership. The fear of failing, the fear of embarrassment, the fear of not knowing what to do, and the fear of thinking I don't have what it takes to lead this team are a few of the fears that come to mind. These can be common fears for a leader. Moving beyond these fears, as Mr. Mandela mentions, is usually a function of admitting that the fear is there and then going on. I often remind myself that even if my worst fear comes true, it will be a learning and growth experience, and so I put my fear behind me and move forward.

Another great lesson in inspiring leadership that I took from Nelson Mandela's life is *humility*. This *is* a word we use when training leaders at IBM. It is very easy to be caught up in the feeling of importance of being an IBM leader. We teach that you will not be successful unless a lot of other people (your team) want you to be. You cannot do it on your own, so think more about your team and less about yourself. Mandela said, "It is better to lead from behind and to put others in front, especially when you celebrate victory when nice things occur. You take the front line when there is danger. Then people will appreciate your leadership." Nelson Mandela is what I would call "others oriented." He never lost sight of the fact that leadership is a people business and that you cannot achieve the great things you want to achieve unless the people around you are all working in that same direction. It has been said that people do things for their reasons, not yours. It is because of this that you need to give people a reason to engage and participate in the process. Helping others to feel that they are valuable and are a necessary part of what you are trying to accomplish will help move you toward the desired goal.

> *It is better to be prepared for an opportunity and not have*
> *one than to have an opportunity and not be prepared.*
> —WHITNEY YOUNG, JR.

Nelson Mandela also can teach us a lot about *focus.* Mandela said, "If there are dreams about a beautiful South Africa, there are also roads that lead to their goal. Two of these roads could be named Goodness and Forgiveness." I will discuss the importance of focus in a later chapter, but for now let me point out that Nelson Mandela had a clear goal of what he wanted to achieve in South Africa. He would not allow bitterness or a lack of forgiveness to distract him from what he dreamed could be accomplished. Mandela had plenty of reasons to hold on to the past and demand justice, but he let his feelings go and kept his focus on the future, and it benefited everyone involved. I heard someone say recently that if you cannot forgive and forget, then choose one.

The thing that impresses me most about Nelson Mandela, and what makes his story an excellent example of inspiring others toward remarkable, is that he could be imprisoned for 27 years and yet upon his release be ready to lead a nation. You would think he would be disconnected and unprepared, but the truth is just the opposite. While in prison, he would do his assigned prison work during the day, and then he would spend his evenings reading and preparing for the future that he envisioned. He led a *balanced and disciplined life* regardless of his circumstances.

This is a teaching point for IBM leaders as well. I often remind our leaders that you cannot give what you do not have, and that if you hope to pour into the lives of others, then you first need to be pouring into yourself. The great lesson here for all of us who aspire to inspire is that people are watching you all the time, and if you are not leading yourself well by being balanced and disciplined, then you can be sure that those watching you will not be positively influenced. I constantly remind IBM leaders that no one wants to follow people who are out of control in their personal or professional life. Develop a disciplined and balanced approach to place yourself in a position to inspire others. I think this is exactly where many leaders miss the on-ramp to being inspirational leaders capable of taking their teams to remarkable performances—they fail to lead balanced and disciplined lives. Many people who are put into leadership positions work hard for a while but then back off over time. They stop doing the things that got them there, thinking that it is enough to just be there. Remarkable and inspiring leaders never stop preparing. Mr. Mandela was well prepared even though he had a terrific excuse to not be prepared.

Inspiring by Admiring

When I tell leaders that they need to inspire their team, I often get a blank look back in return. "How would I do that?" they might ask. "Be inspiring," I tell them. That is easier said than done, I have found. But there are some steps you can take to inspire others, and it is actually easier than you might think.

A young man that I coach once said to me, "I wish I were more like you." Never mind that I am 20 years older than he is and that he did not see any of the struggle or challenge that got me to this point, but he wants to be more like me. I thanked him for the compliment, and we talked about the steps necessary for him to move forward in *his* life. It wasn't until about an hour later that it occurred to me that his comment inspired me to want to be the person that he admired. I found myself

WHY DO WE WANT TO BE INSPIRING LEADERS?

I could see how a leader with all the things he or she has to do might say (or at least think) that all this inspiring leadership stuff is a lot of work—why would I want to do all this? The short answer is that inspirational leaders develop high-performing teams. Here is how the math works:

- Inspirational leaders = inspired followers
- Inspired followers = highly engaged followers
- Highly engaged followers = people who take ownership of the mission
- Owners = people who think for themselves and bring insights to the business
- People who bring insights = people who try new things until they find what works
- People who find what works = people with whom customers really want to work
- Customers who really want to work with you = *a really good thing*

wanting to spend more time with him; I wanted to work harder to help him on his path to success. I found it interesting to note the inspiration I took from his admiration. Then I started to wonder if I could instill that same inspiration in the people on my team if I could communicate my admiration for them and what they do. If you will notice I said my admiration for them *and* what they do, not *or* what they do.

> *I aspire to be half the man my dog thinks I am.*
> —BUMPER STICKER

Focusing Your Admiration

Often as leaders we are quick to show our admiration or appreciation when someone on our team does some task or project well.

We compliment the output, the quality, or the quick turnaround, but we don't necessarily compliment the person. When we are not comfortable showing admiration for someone personally, we can simply focus our praise on what the person has done. To you (the admirer), it feels like you have done a good thing by giving this kind of recognition. To the person (the admired), it feels like you are only pleased with the person when he or she performs well. This leads to a performance-based acceptance relationship with your team. When this occurs, you are communicating more pleasure for the task than for the person, and this develops a belief in the minds of your team members that if they don't keep doing great acts for you, then you will not admire or accept them. Or in employee terms, the boss only admires me because of what I do for the team. What we really want to communicate is how much we admire the *person,* and because of that admiration for the *person,* we are also impressed with what that person can do.

Showing Admiration

Admiration is really a form of respect, and respect communicates value. When I respect you and your opinions and ideas and efforts, I am communicating to you that you are valued. Just a side note from my personal experience: the closer someone is to us relationally, the more likely we take this respect-to-value equation for granted. That was a hard lesson for me when I found that I spent more time and effort showing admiration for the people I worked with than I did for the people I lived with. This principle applies in *every* area of your life; don't miss the obvious application at home.

Developing leaders who can inspire their teams is an important part of the IBM leader development curriculum. One challenge that many young or first-time leaders face is finding the balance between providing direction and communicating value. Sometimes it is the difference between management and leadership. The focus can be so intense on executing the vision each day and providing direction, that it is easy to forget that none of the execution would be possible without the people to do it. The key is to establish a balance between strongly executing the day-to-day tasks and inspiring our people by communicating the value we see in them—this is when we begin to see real advancement toward our goals. Or as one IBM leader told me recently, "The numbers are important, but we cannot forget that there are people behind those numbers." Admiration drives inspiration, and inspiration drives engagement. Engagement is the driving force behind improving performance and achieving remarkable results. Admire your people for who they are *and* what they do.

> *I regard the gift of admiration as indispensable if one is to amount to something; I don't know where I would be without it.*
> —FRANÇOIS DE LA ROCHEFOUCAULD

Once these inexperienced IBM leaders understand the importance of admiration, the question I usually hear is, "How can I communicate admiration and respect to those who work with and for me?" The first lesson you need to embrace is to *ask more than you tell*. Don't you find that you feel admired and valued when people ask you for advice and for your opinion instead of always telling you what they think? When you change your "telling" to "asking," you are saying to the other people that they matter. Ask for their input, and value what they tell you. You don't have to follow all the advice, but when you ask, you communicate respect.

Another great lesson is to *take interest in their interests*. Have you ever felt a sense of admiration when someone takes an interest in what you are interested in? Be careful, however, to make your interest about the *people* doing what they do, not merely about what they do—meaning, if you ask people about their job, make it clear that you really want to know what it is about *them* that makes them love that kind of work. You want to admire *them* for the type of value *they* provide to others. The real lesson here is to *separate the person from the act*. The highest form of admiration is when people admire you for who you are and not just for what you have done.

Finally, take every opportunity you can find to *praise it forward*. Nothing communicates admiration, respect, and value more than hearing that someone was bragging about you. When you praise Bob in front of others, it does two things. First, it raises Bob's value in the eyes of other members of the team. Second, it provides an example to the team of how everyone is expected to communicate. If you said something negative about Bob, the people who heard you say it would wonder what you say about them when they are not present. That would be anti-inspiring leadership. Talk positively and in a praising way in front of others about the people you desire to have a strong relationship with. Somehow it *always* finds its way back to them.

To be esteemed or admired by your family, friends, boss, and coworkers is something that almost every person desires. If you, as the leader, are able to provide esteem to others, then you are giving them a gift that will both inspire and engage them in the work your team is doing. It is a choice you make every time you open your mouth— will you lift others up (inspire), or will you lift yourself up? It is a gift you *choose* to give that, once it is received, will establish a climate for remarkable performances.

CHAPTER 15 POWER POINTS

This chapter has been about becoming an inspiring leader who can consistently lead a team into remarkable performances. Here are the concepts we discussed:

- People are watching you, whether you know it or not. People will do what you do before they will do what you say.
- Becoming an inspiring leader is more about leading from your passion than about any other thing.
- People can become inspired when they believe that you, as the leader, admire them and their ability to contribute to your team.

Leader's Conversation Starter #1

Ask the members of your team to list their three favorite movies and then describe why they have chosen each story. Look for the types of roles they connect with. Are they drawn to:

- ▪ _____ The leader struggling to get things done?
- ▪ _____ The underdog fighting to be heard?
- ▪ _____ The encourager who pushes others to succeed?
- ▪ _____ The villain trying to disrupt and destroy?

Use this as a fun and creative way to help people find what they are passionate about and what inspires them the most.

Leader's Conversation Starter #2

Hand each person on your team several index cards. Then have each person complete one card for every team member (see Figure 15.1). On the card everyone should write the following information:

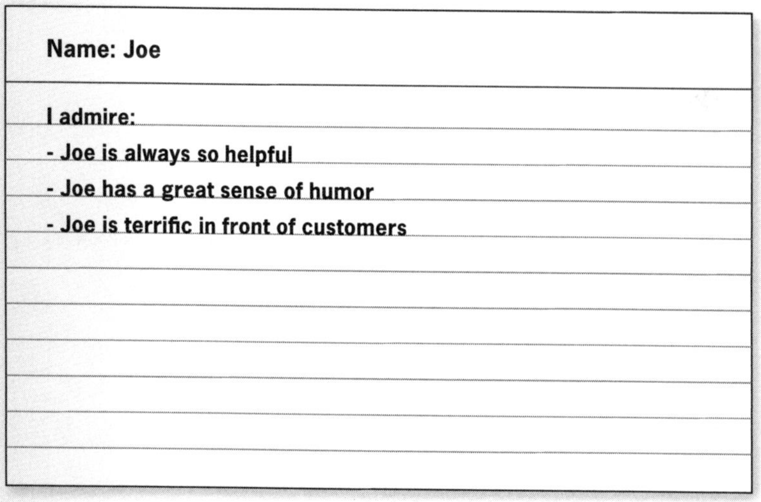

Name: Joe

I admire:
- Joe is always so helpful
- Joe has a great sense of humor
- Joe is terrific in front of customers

FIGURE 15.1 ▪ **The Admiration Card**

- The name of a member of the team (one name per card)
- One to three things they admire most about this person

Collect all the cards and then give each person the cards that were written about them. For a high-impact team meeting, the leader could read aloud one admiration statement that he or she wrote down for each person on the team.

CHAPTER 16

Losing Your Way

Be so good they can't ignore you!

—STEVE MARTIN

No matter where you live around the world, you can't help but notice that it is considered a remarkable feat when your local professional sports club wins the league championship. No matter the sport, when the champ takes home the trophy, we know that it is quite an accomplishment. One question that has always bothered me though is why so few of the teams that win their sports' highest award actually repeat that win the following year. There are very few back-to-back champions. When you look at the last 100+ years of sports competition, no matter what country you are from, there are very few teams that repeat as champions in their league. What makes it so difficult for teams to repeat their remarkable performances?

The answers most people give when asked why professional sports teams have such a difficult time repeating their league championship range from "off-season trades," to "free agency," and to my personal favorite, "everybody's gunning for the champ." Those may all have something to do with the struggles of going back-to-back, but I think there is more to it. Sports teams and corporate teams each face a number of challenges when attempting to repeat a remarkable performance, but the number one challenge that any successful team must face is complacency.

The functionality portion of our Model for Remarkable is about what people see and what that reveals about our ability to deliver and lead remarkable performance in our team or organization. This chapter will uncover some of the ways our pursuit of excellence and our desire for high character can help us avoid the complacency that often accompanies a remarkable performance. Our goal is to develop ourselves and our teams to repeat our remarkable performance, and complacency is a sure way for that not to happen.

The Pride of Having Arrived

My first 10 years with IBM was an amazing time; everything just kind of clicked for the company and for those of us selling at the time. Everyone loved Big Blue, and everyone loved what we sold. Our mainframe computers were the rage, and the software that went with them was king. There was a confidence about buying IBM and knowing your problems would be solved. The personal computer was just an idea on the drawing board, and Microsoft and Intel were just fledgling start-ups. The biggest challenge that IBM leadership had each January was deciding how big a growth target it wanted to set for the coming year. Life was indeed good. And then came the 1990s.

In the early 1990s, after years where IBM enjoyed 14 percent annual compound growth rates, gross profit margins exceeding 60 percent, and a 30 percent market share, the computer industry began to change. The UNIX operating system was released, touting "open" architectures and opening the door for key IBM competitors like Sun Microsystems, Digital Equipment Company, and Hewlett-Packard to compete in ways they were not able to before. By 1993 IBM was on course to report a $16 billion loss. The market had changed, and IBM had failed to change along with it. Even the launch of the era of the personal computer, which IBM helped to invent, was hurting IBM, and IBM was not able to compete effectively. Author Robert Slater, in his book *Saving Big Blue*,[1] gave his opinion of what really happened: "IBM rode high for a long time, but refused to look outside of itself. Management was arrogant to a fault, and when the world of computers began to stampede in a new direction, IBM almost got left in the dust."

From Complacency to Arrogance

A major concern of many leaders is that the people on their team, who are producing remarkable results, will get complacent and stop doing the things they did to be remarkable. As with the IBM story from the 1990s, when things are going well and you are winning, it is human nature to relax and take a little enjoyment for having arrived at this lofty destination. Unfortunately, as we discussed earlier, the real essence of being able to produce remarkable performances is not to back off or slow down; it is to stay focused and continually be adding to your toolkit for providing the next level of remarkable. As we said earlier, what is remarkable today will not be remarkable tomorrow. You have to be intentional about growing and learning to be able to provide the next remarkable performance.

> *When a great team loses through complacency, it will constantly search for new and more intricate explanations to explain away defeat.*
> **—PAT RILEY**

If complacency is allowed to develop, then remarkable gives way to "good enough." When that happens and some success keeps coming your way, arrogance can raise its ugly head, as it did in the IBM example earlier. Can you recover from something like this? Of course you can. IBM did, but it required many very difficult decisions that took years to generate the desired results.

Avoiding Complacency

Although I was young when legendary NFL football coach Vince Lombardi died, I was influenced by his philosophy on life and success. This is probably because American football was the game I played most in my youth and the Vince Lombardi philosophy was always being referenced by either my coach on the field or my dad at home.

COMPLACENCY IS DANGEROUS

The *Merriam-Webster Collegiate Dictionary* defines *complacency* as "self-satisfaction especially when accompanied by unawareness of actual danger or deficiencies." This contentment is dangerous because it can undermine every task or project you or your team engages in.

How can you recognize complacency in yourself or your team? Complacent people are:

- Internally focused
- Not looking to grow or improve
- Fine with the status quo
- Comfortable with "good enough"

As a coach, Lombardi was known for being a tough and demanding man, and his reputation was that of a winner. He inspired remarkable performances from his players. In his time as head coach of the Green Bay Packers, he was able to lead them to five NFL championships and two Super Bowl victories. The championship trophy that the NFL plays for each season is named after him.

When coach Lombardi was asked by the news media what he was going to do to get his team back to the championship games in the coming season, he answered by saying, "We are not going to be flashy. We are going to be brilliant on the basics. We will run, throw, catch, tackle, and block better than every team in the league. That is how we will go to the championships this year."

What Coach Lombardi knew is that success often breeds carelessness and complacency. Once we taste victory or enjoy a winning season, we tend to adopt an attitude of complacency. "I have made it... I have arrived... I can relax." I saw this characteristic in myself early in my career. When I was first assigned to a customer account in our sales territory, I would diligently plan and prepare before any sales call that was scheduled. I gave myself homework every night so that I would not let the team down the following day as we worked with that customer.

Then a funny thing happened—I was successful. I made the One-Hundred-Percent Club; I won the trip to Miami. The following year I didn't have homework any longer. Did I not have important customer meetings any longer? No, of course I did; I felt that I could wing it now because, well, I had arrived. I had done all this before. I knew how it worked. I didn't need to work so hard to get by any longer.

I find this to be one of the biggest reasons why we have so few repeat champions and why our performances drop off from one year to the next; we become enamored with our own success, and we become complacent. We don't say those words out loud; we hardly even notice it is happening. We make one seemingly insignificant choice to cut a corner, and then tomorrow we make another seemingly insignificant choice to cut another corner, and before you know it, we are miles from where we intended to be. If you ever played in the ocean as a kid and looked up to see you were no longer in front of the beach chairs where your parents were sitting, you know how this feels. We think we are in one place and don't even realize we have drifted with the currents to a place we did not intend to be. Whether you are selling, leading, teaching, or parenting, being brilliant on the basics is what places you in the position to win day after day, month after month, and year after year after year.

Finding Your Fundamentals

Speaker and author Jeffrey Gitomer wrote[2] that he was tired of hearing people say they needed to return to the basics as a solution to every sales problem the organization was having. He claimed that people have no idea what that means and that what we need to return to is *reality*. That article got me thinking about what it is that Coach Lombardi really meant when he said that for his players to return to the championship games, they would need to be brilliant on the basics. What Coach Lombardi understood is that you cannot get to the level of repeating remarkable performances if you don't stay focused on the fundamental execution of your craft, whatever that craft may be. The reality of providing consistently remarkable performances for your customer means that you need to be solid on the fundamentals of your craft and then move beyond the basics of doing your craft. You cannot deliver remarkable for your client if you *only* do the basics, but without knowing and doing the fundamentals, you will be tempted to cut corners that will lead to a letdown in your intensity and execution. My experience is that you need to be brilliant on the fundamentals and then move beyond the basics of your craft to provide remarkable service for your client—although being "brilliant on the fundamentals" does not roll off your tongue as nicely as "brilliant on the basics."

In football, Coach Lombardi said, "Some people try to find things in this game that don't exist but football is only two things—blocking and tackling." This can be true of all of us: we can focus on things that are not important or are not relevant to our overall success or to the solutions our customers are looking for us to provide. In the story of IBM in the 1990s, the new CEO, Louis Gerstner, and his leadership team began to cut away things that had nothing to do with what they believed to be IBM's fundamental business. I was surprised to read that some of the cuts included most of the corporate jets IBM had amassed and a fine art collection that went for $31 million. Both items were nice to have I guess, but they have nothing to do with the fundamental business of solving customer information technology issues. What Gerstner learned was that the fundamentals for IBM were its culture and its customer focus. When he recognized that truth, he was able to use those strong fundamentals to move IBM away from products (mostly hardware at the time) to solutions that would combine hardware, software, and services. The move placed IBM on a road to recovery that was focused on doing a few fundamentals really well.

Because I am a professional trainer and speaker, the fundamentals for me are *preparation* and *confidence*. I have found that the more I prepare, the more confidence I have. If I shortcut the preparation because I have given this speech before, I risk going on stage with less confidence than I might normally have. Then if one person in the audience decides to be provocative and ask a challenging question, I might stumble or be unconvincing in my response. I doubt anyone will leave that room saying, "Wow! That was a remarkable session."

The question to ask yourself at this point is, what are the fundamentals for you? Have you stepped away from them and allowed your focus to be on things that have nothing to do with the remarkable performances that you and your team desire to deliver? Here is a short exercise (see Figure 16.1) to help you identify and evaluate your grasp of the fundamentals in your business:

1. Identify three key fundamentals for your line of work. What is it that really successful people in your area of expertise do day after day better than anyone else?
2. Perform an honest self-evaluation on these basics. Do a simple low = 1 (I did not know that this was one of my fundamentals), high = 10 (I am doing really well in this area) evaluation

---

"Remarkable-Me Moment"—Personal Evaluation

What are three fundamentals for your line of work. What is it that really successful people do day after day better than anyone else? How would you rate yourself?

1 = low; 10 = high

Fundamental #1: _____ _____

Fundamental #2: _____ _____

Fundamental #3: _____ _____

Fundamental #1: Action Planner (what do I need to do today to begin improving on this?)

_____

_____

Fundamental #2: Action Planner

_____

_____

Fundamental #2: Action Planner

_____

_____

FIGURE 16.1 ▪ Know Your Fundamentals

3. Identify one or two actions you could take in each fundamental area to begin to strengthen your abilities there.
4. Set aside a few minutes each day to execute on that plan. (Read, practice, study, think.)

Coach Lombardi said, "Success demands singleness of purpose." It is very easy for us to be distracted by the flashy, high-visibility tasks that grab our attention and impress others. We often take for granted the small, seemingly insignificant things that we should be doing consistently every day. These are the things that ultimately compound to drive our success and put us on the road to remarkable.

Coach Lombardi also said, "The only place success comes before work is in the dictionary." It is also easy to wish and want for success without being willing to put in the work required to actually be successful. I wish I could play the piano like my daughter, but I did not spend any time seated at the keys today doing the exercises that she did to deepen her skill. I wish I could hit a golf ball like Tiger Woods. But am I willing to hit 1,000 balls a day, rain or shine, like he does? Many will say they want to be excellent at what they do, but very few are willing to put in the hard work of becoming excellent. Are you?

Going from Fundamental to Remarkable

Doing something that is worthy of remark from someone else means moving past the fundamentals and really developing the discipline of excellence. I hesitate to use the word *discipline* because it can be taken in a negative way. Your dad said he was going to discipline you when he got home. Your coach told you that you needed to be more disciplined, and that meant running extra wind sprints after practice. The word *discipline* can bring up bad memories for a lot of us.

When I say the *discipline of excellence*, I mean it to be an exercise or activity that develops the skills that lead to remarkable in everything you do. This means that you have to identify the things that lead to average performance and replace those activities with things that result in remarkable. You need a plan to hold yourself accountable for what you are saying you want to accomplish. Knowing how easy it is to cut corners and how easy it is to become complacent, you need to ensure that you become intentional about doing what you say you are going to do.

CHAPTER 16 POWER POINTS

In this chapter we have taken a closer look at how you can strengthen the functionality layer of the Model for Remarkable by avoiding the tendency of successful teams to lose their way when it comes to delivering or even repeating remarkable performances. Some of the Power Points to remember are:

- How to avoid the pride of having arrived
- What steps to take to avoid falling into complacency
- How to become brilliant on the fundamentals

Leader's Conversation Starter

As we close this chapter, I would like to ask you to take a moment and think about actions you need to take to keep from losing your way on the path to delivering and repeating remarkable performances. If you are in a position to lead others into remarkable performances, you might want to consider leading your team members through this exercise to record their actions.

The biggest challenge for individuals and teams that want to achieve and repeat remarkable performances is to overcome the lure of complacency. Either on your own or with your team, complete the exercise in Figure 16.2. For each of the statements, use the following grading system:

1 = Yes, the statement is true for me.
2 = Sometimes the statement is true for me.
3 = No, the statement is not true for me.

For each group of questions, total the score, and then for the entire set of questions, calculate your grand total. You may then place the grand total on the scale at the bottom to determine if you should be concerned about complacency in yourself or in your team. If you find that you are creeping into the complacency zone, then return to the chapter to review what can be done to avoid this very dangerous place.

Rate yourself on a scale of 1–3, where 1 = yes, 2 = sometimes, 3 = no.

Fundamentals: **Total**
- ■ I return to the fundamentals on every project.
- ■ I refuse to take shortcuts, even when others insist.
- ■ I never stop at "good enough."

Time: **Total**
- ■ I spend some time every day working on my skills.
- ■ I believe I have a lot to learn.
- ■ I spend at least 30 minutes a day reading in my area of expertise.

Attitude: **Total**
- ■ I am rarely ever satisfied that we have done our best.
- ■ I would never wing it on a customer visit.
- ■ I feel I can always prepare more.

Grand Total

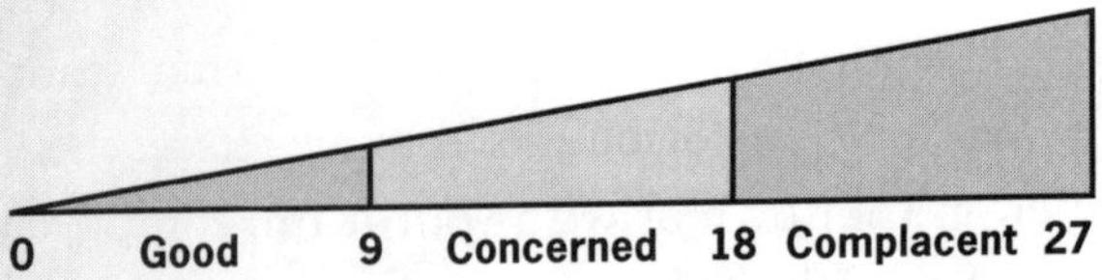

0   Good   9   Concerned   18   Complacent   27

FIGURE 16.2 ■ The Complacency Zone

CHAPTER 17

Focus, Focus, Focus

Focus is a matter of deciding what things you're not going to do.
—JOHN CARMACK

IT WAS pouring rain as I prepared to leave my hotel in Seattle. The rain was so heavy that I offered to bring the rental car around to the front of the hotel to pick up the consultant with whom I was traveling. As I pulled in front of the hotel, he was nowhere to be seen, and so I parked the car and went into the hotel lobby to look for him. About this time a tour bus with over 100 tourists had arrived, and all of them were in the lobby, and all of them were talking—at the same time... all of them... talking. It took me a few minutes to locate my colleague standing in the middle of the lobby, his suitcase and computer bag propped against his leg, a newspaper in his hand. He was deeply focused on some article in the newspaper. He was so engrossed in what he was reading that I did not want to interrupt him, and so I took the suitcase and computer bag to the car; it's just the kind of guy that I am.

After waiting a few minutes more, I returned to the lobby to see him still reading his paper in the midst of these 100 tourists all talking... at the same time. Did I already mention that? I was ready to go, so I went over and tapped him on the shoulder and pointed toward the car. It was then that he looked down and noticed his suitcase was gone, and, more important, his computer case was missing. He immediately began to scream that his bag had been stolen. Up until that point I would have bet you money that you could not make all those tourist be quiet. I would have lost money. As the lobby got very quiet,

I quickly calmed my friend and pushed him toward the car where all his belongings were safely stored away.

Most people have no idea of the giant capacity we can immediately command when we focus all of our resources on mastering a single area of our lives.
—TONY ROBBINS

As we drove away from the hotel, I began to question him on how he could have *possibly* been able to focus on what he was reading in the midst of the mayhem of the hotel lobby. How could he be so engrossed that he would not notice me taking his bag? I can't read a newspaper in a library without looking up two or three times a minute to see what everyone else is doing. My friend explained to me how he learned the skill of concentration and focus when he was in elementary school. Now I was really intrigued—he called it a skill. I had never considered this something you can learn. It turns out that when he was a student in school, his family owned a seamstress shop in a house in a busy downtown area. The family home was upstairs from the shop, and the ladies who did the sewing worked in a room where my friend went to do his homework each day. He told me that there were three or four seamstresses shouting over the noise of their sewing machines to carry on a conversation with one another. The room was divided by a curtain, and my friend was on the other side of the curtain doing his studies. If my parents had placed me in a locked room with no windows, I would have found a way to be distracted from my studies. My friend was forced to learn to focus on what he was there to accomplish and not let the other activities and noises that surrounded him keep him from his goal.

One of the greatest requirements in the functionality of our Model for Remarkable, and something that others see whether you do or don't, is focus. If you have it, people know it, and they develop a confidence that will open the door to remarkable. If you don't have focus, you can pretty much dismiss any thoughts of getting to remarkable.

Developing the Skill of Focus

TV newscaster Diane Sawyer was once asked about what she considered to be the secret to her success. She replied, "I think the one lesson I've learned is there is no substitute for paying attention." In our hustle and hurry world of overbooked calendars and multitasking activities, this ability to concentrate is a skill that has been pushed away and forgotten. In the years since that experience in Seattle, I became determined to practice this skill every chance I got so that I could increase my effectiveness in the work that I do. This is still a challenge for me. I am still way too aware of all that is going on around me. Why is focusing difficult for me—and for so many others?

I think the problem stems from our high-tech world, and it is only increasing in intensity. When I was young, there were only a few technologies to distract you, like TV and radio. Today the pull of technologies is growing exponentially with every passing year. I was in a restaurant not too long ago, and I witnessed a table of eight young people waiting for their meal to be served. They all had their phones or PDAs either out on the table within their reach or actually in their hands checking their e-mail, their text messages, their Facebook wall, their Twitter feed, and who knows what else. Not one of them was speaking to another person at the table. They probably sent a text message to ask for the salt and pepper.

The busyness of our schedules had added another level of intensity to our lives and another distraction to the mix. We have been taught that in order to be productive we *have* to multitask. As I mentioned earlier in the book, multitasking is a quick way to nonproductivity. Yet we do it without a second thought.

Focus on Focusing

As Mr. Han, the kung fu teacher in the Hollywood movie *The Karate Kid,* liked to tell his young student, "Your focus needs more focus." I believe that in order to be the best we can be and be capable of delivering remarkable performances, we need to increase our ability to focus.

If you want to differentiate yourself from others, learn the skill of focus and concentration.

In leadership training at IBM, we have found that the ability to focus is a key component of successful leaders. Sometimes it is assumed that leaders at this level come to the job with a strong ability to focus; however, what we find is that it is a skill that needs constant care and feeding. To do that, we teach a few fundamentals of learning and maintaining the ability to focus.

The first step in developing a strong ability to focus is to *have a plan*. This is why the foundation for our Model for Remarkable is so important. We must know *what* we are trying to accomplish and have a plan to get there. When I find myself struggling to focus, I can usually track my problem to not having a clear plan for what I am trying to do. A plan does not need to be some big formal thing, but merely an understanding of what you want to accomplish in the time allotted. When I do not lay out the specific outcome I desire to achieve, I can find myself jumping from task to task with nothing much to show for all my effort. A vague plan or no plan allows my mind to wander.

The next thing you need to do to increase your ability to focus is to *break projects into smaller, well-defined parts*. The larger the project that you are trying to accomplish, the more likely it is that you will feel overwhelmed from time to time. This feeling of being overwhelmed

YOUR FOCUS NEEDS MORE FOCUS

The ability to focus is a skill that can be learned. To build this skill you must be intentional and purposeful about making focus a priority. To develop the skill of focus, establish these practices in your life:

1. Learn to say no to interruptions.
2. Establish time blocks to perform your work.
3. Work to extend your time blocks to 90 minutes.
4. Don't answer your phone every time it rings.
5. Don't check your e-mail first thing in the morning.

can lead to distraction and lack of focus. Instead of trying to consume the elephant in one bite, break it into bite-size chunks so you can more easily schedule and complete portions of the project with greater focus. My first task in writing this book was to lay out the chapters and then work on them one at the time.

Once you have defined all the parts of the project or task you are trying to accomplish, you need to *prioritize the chunks*. Whether it is the bits and pieces of a small project or the bite-size chunks from a larger project, prioritize the things you need to get done. Ensure that you are always working on the most important things first. If you are working on one task while a bigger, more important task has not been completed, you will not be able to give the smaller tasks the level of focus needed to deliver remarkable. When you handle the big rocks first (discussed earlier), it helps you to clear your mind so you can focus and know that you are doing exactly what you are supposed to be doing.

Another thing that you can do to increase focus is to *set a start and stop time*. Letting projects ramble on with no defined starts and stops is a recipe for distraction. When you schedule a certain amount of time to work on one thing, you will find that it becomes easier for you to focus on that one thing. If distractions appear, you learn that you can push them off until the scheduled end time for the current activity. Without defined times, you can easily jump from one thing to another and never really provide the necessary focus. Author Tony Schwartz, in his book *Be Excellent at Anything*, says, "Work not only expands to fill the time allotted to it, but it also contracts to fit within the time allotted to it."[1]

When IBM leaders struggle with maintaining a strong ability to focus, it is usually due to the many distractions that try to vie for their attention. These distractions can come as physical distractions and mental distractions. Here is how the great leaders at IBM manage to handle each.

Distract Me and I Will Follow You Anywhere

Physical distractions are things like a noisy work environment or a high-activity area. An example would be an environment where children are running though the house or colleagues at work are walking, talking, and hovering around your cubicle or office. This could be any physical workspace that provides a lot of moving or noisy things to grab your attention; *choose your work area wisely* and have a defined place where you can do your work. This needs to be away from high-traffic and high-noise areas. If you cannot move your work area, you should consider how you arrange your workspace. I like to place my desk facing a wall when a lot of people have theirs facing the middle of the room. I can turn my chair to face visitors, but I do not want all the activity outside my door to catch my attention.

Another step that many leaders take to reduce distraction is to *keep their work area clear* of items that distract. Distracting items could be a phone, e-mail or social media applications, family photos, or desktop play toys, just to name a few. You know what they are. Put the things somewhere else and turn off the technology. Silence all notification alarms. There was a time in my office that you could hear three alarms announcing the arrival of one e-mail. My smartphone would buzz, my iPad would chirp, and my laptop would chime. My wife said it sounded like an orchestra warming up. No wonder focus is a challenge. So, to repeat, turn off all notification alerts. E-mail, Twitter, Facebook, and the rest, can all wait until you are at an appropriate stopping point. This will give you an increased chance at successfully focusing on the important tasks at hand.

Even Worse—Mental Distractions

The wandering mind can be infinitely more distracting than the physical distractions that were mentioned above. You can move away from the physical stuff, but your brain stays with you most of the time. Because I know that my mind will drift to other things, I have developed some tactics to help me deal with these types of mental distractions.

The first and most important thing you can do to avoid or minimize mental distractions is to *remember the schedule you have set.* You should remind yourself that you have allotted a specific amount of time for this effort and that you are going to focus until the scheduled time to stop. This sounds a little hokey, but knowing that you will be free to think about other things in an hour and a half really does make a difference. Contrast this to jumping from one project to something else every time you have a thought pop into your mind to remember to call someone or to not forget to do this or that. Knowing you will get to it in due time helps you to let it go for now and focus.

Another seemingly insignificant step is to *keep a notepad handy.* I always place a blank pad and pen next to my work area. When a distracting thought comes along, I write it down, and then I let the thought go. It is amazing how much better you can concentrate once your brain knows that you have captured the distracting thought. Not writing it down keeps it floating around in your head and telling your brain over and over to not forget. This is especially true when you set time aside to read. It never fails that when you are reading, something you know you need not to forget comes to mind. Before developing these tactics, I would stop what I was reading and do what I was hoping not to forget to do. Now I reach over to my trusty pad, make a note, and then go straight back to reading. With my mind no longer trying to not forget something, I read better, and I have better comprehension of what I have read.

Break for Focus

If, after taking these steps, you are still struggling to focus, you may just need to *take a break.* You could take a short walk or just stand and stretch for a few minutes. Going outside is best if that is possible, but any form of stepping away, even if only for a few minutes, will work. Just get away from the work for 10 minutes or so to refresh yourself and regain the right perspective. Turning to another project and calling it a break is not acceptable. That's multitasking. This is called "being distracted" and exactly what we are trying to improve on. Step away, refresh yourself, and then come back to the project with a renewed mind.

If you are a parent of small children, I encourage you to begin training in the area of focus now. As a father myself, I have seen the incredible battle for the attention of our young people. Distractions come from every direction and use technology to the max. As I noted, when I was young, it was TV and radio; today it is a 24-hour news cycle and technology that never sleeps. Recognize now that focus is a skill and that if it is not practiced, it will not develop. The skill of focus can be learned and mastered with the right amount of practice and patience.

CHAPTER 17 POWER POINTS

In this chapter we have taken a closer look at how the functionality of your Model for Remarkable will never be complete if you do not develop your skill of focus. When it comes to delivering or even repeating remarkable performances, being able to focus your efforts and attention is an invaluable skill to possess. To develop your skill of focus, remember to:

- Have a defined plan of attack
- Break your plan into smaller, manageable pieces
- Prioritize the pieces
- Set start and stop times
- Manage and eliminate distractions—mental and physical

Areas to Consider	I Will Start Doing	I Will Stop Doing	I Will Keep Doing
To help me to increase my ability to focus . . .			
To help me plan and prioritize my work . . .			
To deal with physical and mental distractions . . .			

FIGURE 17.1 ■ Leader's Conversation Starter

If you are in a position to lead others into remarkable performances, you might want to consider leading the people on your team through the exercise in Figure 17.1 to record their actions. For each area mentioned in the figure, make a note of any actions you need to *start* doing, *stop* doing, or *keep* doing. These may be small, seemingly insignificant choices you must make to be remarkable, or they may be bigger measures that you know you need to incorporate as a regular part of your personal strategy going forward. When you are able to make these choices on a consistent basis over time, you will positively compound your remarkable results.

CHAPTER 18

From Remarkable to Memorable

Life doesn't get easier or more forgiving; we
get stronger and more resilient.

—STEVE MARABOLI

IN HER bestselling book *Unbroken: A World War II Story of Survival, Resilience, and Redemption,*[1] author Laura Hillenbrand tells the story of Louis Zamperini. Zamperini was a bombardier on a B-24 bomber during World War II when the plane went down in the Pacific Ocean. Zamperini survived the crash along with two others and set off on an incredible journey that included 47 days at sea with very little to eat or drink, capture by the Japanese and imprisonment in one POW camp after another, repeated torture and beatings, and finally rescue and return to the United States. It is a remarkable story about a remarkable man. And now, after 70 years since the time his plane ditched, he is not only remarkable but memorable as well.

The characteristic that most amazes me about the Louis Zamperini story, and what I believe allows him to bridge the gap between remarkable and memorable, is the *resilience* he exhibited in the face of unbelievable challenge. If you look up the definition of the word *resilience,*[2] you will see it described as the ability to recover from or adjust easily to misfortune or change. Louis Zamperini did that and more. What moves someone from being remarkable to being memorable is the ability to consistently and repeatedly deliver remarkable performance and be able to recover from or adjust easily to misfortune or change.

A good half of the art of living is resilience.
—ALAIN DE BOTTON

Remarkably Resilient

Woody Allen once said, "Eighty percent of success is showing up." That may be true, but 100 percent of remarkable is having the character quality of resilience. After all you have learned about the Model for Remarkable and the foundation, the framework, and the functionality, it will all be meaningless if you do not possess the ability to adapt to constantly changing conditions. You can never develop the ability to consistently deliver remarkable performances if you do not recognize the implications of being resilient or teach your team how to be resilient in the face of the challenges and changes that define most of the projects that are worth doing.

Do not let what you cannot do interfere with what you can do.
—JOHN WOODEN

For IBM to have celebrated its one hundredth birthday, some resilience had to be involved. If you consider the changes in the technology, the changes in competition, the changes in global markets, and the changes in networking capabilities, you can easily see how an organization with little or no capacity for resiliency would not be here today. The company may get credit for being here for 100 years, but it has been the resilient nature of the people of IBM that made the real difference. To be able to keep going when things were difficult, to keep looking for answers to customer problems as economies changed, and to keep growing as technologies were born, matured, and died requires this special capacity to be resilient in the face of whatever comes your way.

To develop this incredible quality of resilience, I recommend that the leaders of IBM, and your organization, work with their teams to develop three traits that will enable them to take on and then move past the challenges that so easily derail many performances. The first character quality that you need to make sure your people embrace if you hope to remain positioned for a remarkable performance is *flexibility*.

Many times you see people become utterly determined in their mind that their way to accomplish a task is the *only* way to accomplish that task. When challenge or change is presented to them, they grasp their ideas and hold on for dear life, oftentimes riding those ideas right into an average or mediocre result. Remaining flexible does not mean that you give up on your ideas the first time a challenge is presented, but that you remain open to other ways of doing things. Even though you are always confident that your ideas are the ones to get you to where you want the team to be, you may want to adapt an "all of us are smarter than one of us" approach to leading your team. This means that you include and listen to others who are involved with you in solving a problem. Many a performance has gone down in flames when the leader held on to a certain way of doing things and refused to be flexible in the face of challenge and change.

Another character quality of resilient people that we ask IBM leaders to embrace is the ability to be *adaptable*. Where flexible is about bending where and when you need to bend while performing a task, adaptable is about changing course when necessary while performing a task. I have seen a leadership change in the customer organization throw a potentially remarkable project into turmoil because my team leader would not adapt to the new personality and opinions of the new customer executive. It appeared to be some sort of battle of the wills from which neither person was willing to back down. Being adaptable says that you are able to make adjustments to your approach when conditions change or challenges present themselves. People who are unable to adapt are locked in to repeating unsuccessful approaches and have no chance of being resilient.

The third character quality of a resilient person or team is the ability to be *stretchable*. I am not sure that is a real word, but it describes perfectly what I think is an undeniable character quality of remarkable performers. Stretchable means that you are always learning and developing, stretching your insight and understanding of how you can improve and grow. Where *flexible* is about bending your approach to a project when conditions change, *stretchable* is more about how you personally grow and develop during each project. Resilient people see everything as a learning experience. Being able to stretch yourself is the pathway to increasing your personal value and opening the door to many remarkable performances. If people refuse to stretch and grow, they will repeat the mistakes that restricted previous performances, and they are doomed to be average or worse.

Coach Thyself

When my son was young, he decided to play baseball. He was quite good and quickly earned a starting position on every team he joined. I would spend hours in the front yard throwing the ball with him and even more time at the ballpark watching him play. While at the ballpark, I was amazed at the number of fathers who would scream over the fence during the game to tell their sons what they needed to do. "Keep your eye on the ball!" "Keep your head down and follow through." "Pay attention, Billy!" The kids were embarrassed, but the fathers were insistent that all their kids needed was a bit of coaching.

When seasons changed, my son decided to join a tennis league and play competitively with a few of his friends. An interesting thing happened when we arrived for the first tennis match; parents were told they could not offer any verbal "encouragement" of any kind. They were allowed to politely clap after every point; nothing else. It took about 90 seconds for the yelling fathers from the baseball park to be asked to remain quiet or leave the stadium. As my son and I were driving home from a tennis match, I asked him what he thought about the "parents must be quiet" rule. He told me that it was wonderful not to have to listen to Billy's dad screaming at Billy, but he wished he could come to the fence and ask me for some coaching during the match like we did when he played baseball.

The next week my son was involved in an extremely tough match, and he was struggling to find a way to score against his opponent. After the match, he repeated what he had told me earlier, that he wished he could have come to me for some coaching. Since we had spent hours and hours talking tennis, I asked him what he thought I would have told him he should do. He thought about that for a minute and then told me three things he thought I would have coached him to do in that situation. I told him the next time he was in trouble that he should look at me in the stands and that I would hold up one hand formed in the shape of the letter C. That would be my reminder to him to "coach thyself." He smiled and began to realize that most of the time all we really need to do is take a step back and think for a minute of the options that we should consider in this situation.

What I was specifically asking my son to do was exactly what we teach IBM managers to do when we ask them to coach their teams. We want our leaders to spend time providing input to their teams, with the hope that with more and more input from their boss, the individual team members will soon be able to coach themselves when the boss is not available.

The approach we train our leaders to use is called GROW, and it is a very well-known business tool that I just happen to think can be used to solve everyday problems. It goes like this:

- *G—goal.* What is your desired outcome? Your goal? What are you trying to accomplish?
- *R—reality.* What is your current reality? Where are you starting from?
- *O—options.* What are some things you could try? What are your options for moving forward?
- *W—way forward.* Of the options you listed, what will you choose? What actions will you now take?

If you can instill a GROW mindset in yourself and your team, there will come a point where you can simply hold up your hand in the shape of a C and ask the people on your team how they would coach themselves in this situation.

Coaching still remains a central tenet of the IBM leadership training model. It also remains a constant struggle for most leaders; this is not because they don't think it is important—they do! They struggle with it because they believe that it takes time to be a great coach, and time is the one thing we cannot produce more of. One way that I have found to counter this perception of needing more time is to help our leaders move from coaching as yet another task on their already lengthy to-do list to having a culture of coaching in their organization. To make this point I describe the typical day of a first-line manager in terms of a pizza—lots of different slices, and I will get to them, slice by slice, as time and urgency allow. Coaching is one of my many slices, and I will get to it when I have time... and I almost never have time.

Developing a coaching culture means not viewing coaching as another slice to be dealt with, but viewing coaching as the crust under every slice. This means that when I am working in the "sales calls with my team" slice, I look for an opportunity to provide a little coaching to my team. When I am in the "pipeline review" slice with my team, I look for the opportunity to provide a little coaching. Taking this culture of coaching approach begins to open up many more opportunities for us to provide feedback and encourage the people who work for us. In my area of IBM, we are trying this approach to help move away from heavy inspection, which adds very little value to an individual's ability to execute, to a coaching discussion that will help the execution move forward more swiftly.

Six Amazing Actions to Take with Your Team

In order for you to be remarkable and for you to lead remarkable, you will need a team of players who can coach themselves in the middle of the battle. To build a culture and environment for moving from remarkable to memorable, I recommend the following six amazing actions you can take with your team:

1. Spend time getting to know every individual on your team personally. Who are these individuals? What makes them tick? What are they passionate about?
2. Ensure that all the team members know their own roles on the team and the importance of their contribution to what the team is trying to accomplish.
3. Celebrate setbacks publicly by communicating the lessons learned and the steps to take the next time those situations occur.
4. Encourage and publicly recognize personal growth and improvement by members of your team.
5. Encourage ownership and autonomy with each member of your team.
6. Encourage the consistent flow of feedback between you and every member of your team. What's working? What needs to be improved?

I have noticed on my own teams over the years that taking these six actions helps to break down any walls that might normally form that restrict the ability to deliver remarkable. By taking these six actions, you will increase the engagement of every person on your team. Increasing engagement increases performance, and that leads you toward remarkable.

Questions That Remarkable Leaders Ask

As we conclude our journey about leading and delivering remarkable performances, I want to leave you with the following list of questions that remarkable leaders must ask to ensure they consistently deliver remarkable and then move from remarkable to memorable.

1. What is the desired outcome of this project or engagement in the view of our customers?

2. Why is the outcome important to our customers or audiences? What is the impact to their business or their people?

3. What is our point of view in this situation or project of what will help the customers achieve their desired outcome?

4. What insight can we bring to this project or engagement that might help the customers see things in a way they may not have considered previously?

5. What are the things we can do to develop and maintain trust with these clients?

6. What is our unique value, and how will it be exhibited during this project or engagement?

7. What is our daily, weekly, and monthly plan for continued personal growth and development?

8. What should we be doing that we are not doing that would cause our customers to say, "Wow!"?

9. What have we learned about ourselves during this project or engagement that we may not have been aware of before? How will it help us to improve our performance?

10. What will we do differently on the next project or engagement, based on what we have learned?

I think you will agree that when you can develop the intentional approach to communicating with your team and asking the questions listed above, you will open the door for many remarkable performances. A critical mistake that leaders often make is in not intentionally communicating their message to their team. We get busy, we think everyone knows what should be done, and when they don't we deliver poor performances. Take the time to make a plan for how you will communicate with your team and do not leave the door to average performance open even a crack. The things that need to be done to be remarkable are easy to do; unfortunately, they are also easy *not* to do.

CHAPTER 18 POWER POINTS

In this chapter we looked at the importance of being resilient if you hope to be able to move from remarkable to memorable in your performance. The components of a resilient character are:

- Flexibility
- Adaptability
- Stretchability

We also spoke about developing the ability to "coach thyself" while in the middle of the game, and we gave thought to how this skill enables remarkable performance.

We concluded the chapter with six amazing actions to take and the 10 questions that remarkable leaders ask.

Leader's Conversation Starter

To assist you and your team in developing the character quality of resilience, have each person answer the following questions and then discuss them together as a team:

1. I can be very flexible in executing my plan for a particular project.

_____ TRUE _____ FALSE

If false, why is this, and what can you do to become more flexible in working with others?_____

_____

_____

_____

2. I adapt well to changing situations.

_____ TRUE _____ FALSE

If false, why is this, and what can you do to become more adaptable when working conditions change?_____

_____

_____

_____

3. I often stretch myself by taking on new challenges that will help
me grow and develop.
_____ TRUE   _____ FALSE
If false, why is this, and what can you do to allow yourself to
stretch more?_____

_____

_____

NOTES

Preface

1. From Wikipedia, http://en.wikipedia.org/wiki/Cirque_du_Soleil.

Introduction

1. *It's Your Ship,* copyright 2002, D. Michael Abrashoff, Warner Business Books.
2. From Dictionary.com, http://dictionary.reference.com/browse/remarkable.

Chapter 2

1. http://www.foodnetwork.com/restaurant-impossible/index.html.
2. *The 21 Irrefutable Laws of Leadership*, copyright 1998, John C. Maxwell, Thomas Nelson Publishing.
3. http://www.ikea.com/us/en/.

Chapter 3

1. I have also read John Maxwell talking about a similar idea of balancing care with candor in his book *The Five Levels of Leadership*, copyright 2011, John Maxwell, Hachette Book Group.
2. *Crucial Conversations,* copyright 2002, Kerry Patterson, Joseph Grenny, Ron McMillan, and Al Switzler, McGraw-Hill.

Chapter 4

1. IBM Values Jam, http://www.ibm.com/ibm/values/us/.
2. https://www.collaborationjam.com/.
3. http://online.wsj.com/article/SB100014240527023048409045774226837648666606.html.

Chapter 5

1. *The Principle of the Path: How to Get from Where You Are to Where You Want to Be*, copyright 2008, Andy Stanley, Thomas Nelson Publishers.

Chapter 6

1. *The Compound Effect,* copyright 2010, Success Media, Darren Hardy, Vanguard Press.
2. *The Compound Effect,* p. 69.
3. *Failing Forward: Turning Mistakes into Stepping Stones for Success,* copyright 2000, John Maxwell, Maxwell Motivation, Inc., Thomas Nelson Publishers.
4. http://www-05.ibm.com/employment/ie/insidesales/insidesales_and_you/sales.shtml.

Chapter 7

1. http://www.stellaawards.com/.
2. http://www.stellaawards.com/bogus.html.
3. http://www.laraequy.com/blog/.

Chapter 8

1. Thanks to Josh Davis of Proskuneo Ministries (http://www.proskuneo .info) for helping me with this great explanation of diligence.

Chapter 9

1. *The War of Art,* copyright 2002, Steven Pressfield, Grand Central Publishing.
2. *The War of Art*, p. 62.

Chapter 10

1. http://www.usatoday.com/news/health/story/2012-06-11/sleep-stroke-risk/55506530/1?csp=34news.
2. http://www.youtube.com/watch?v=Wu5Dn4uCau8.
3. I have heard this in several different places, but my first experience with this method came from Brian Tracy.

Chapter 11

1. http://www.the register.co.uk/2011/03/10/ibm_investor_day_2011
   _palmisano/.

Chapter 13

1. http://en.wikipedia.org/wiki/Hall_of_fame.

Chapter 15

1. http://money.cnn.com/2011/06/20/news/economy/workers_disgruntled/
   index.htm.
2. *The Inspiring Leader: Unlocking the Secrets of How Extraordinary Leaders Motivate*, copyright 2009, Jack Zenger, Joe Folkman, Scott Edinger, McGraw-Hill.

Chapter 16

1. *Saving Big Blue*, copyright 1999, Robert Slater, McGraw-Hill.
2. http://www.gitomer.com/articles/ViewPublicArticle.html?key=ajcdMibak
   3NA4sKEiT12Uw%3D%3D.

Chapter 17

1. *Be Excellent at Anything*, copyright 2010, Tony Schwartz, Free Press, a division of Simon & Schuster.

Chapter 18

1. *Unbroken: A World War II Story of Survival, Resilience, and Redemption*, copyright 2010, Laura Hillenbrand, Random House.
2. http://www.merriam-webster.com/dictionary/resilience.

INDEX

ABOUT THE AUTHOR

PERRY HOLLEY is a native of Santa Monica, California, but grew up in the Cape Canaveral area of Florida, where his father worked in spaceflight operations. A graduate of the University of Georgia, Perry earned his degree in business at the Terry School of Business at UGA in Athens. Perry is a motivational and personal devclopment speaker and trainer for the IBM Corporation, specializing in leadership, selling, and personal effectiveness.

Perry has a background in sales and sales leadership. He has led sales teams for IBM and for other companies as well. He has served clients in both large global organizations and smaller, new business territories. He has a passion for developing others and seeing people grow into the leaders they were intended to be.

Perry and his wife of 30+ years, Bonnie, have two children and live in Atlanta.

You may follow and stay connected to Perry at:

Website, http://www.perryholley.com
Twitter, http://www.twitter.com/perryholley
YouTube, http://www.youtube.com/perryholley
Facebook, http://www.facebook.com/perrymholley